Unwea

the Web

Deception and Adaptation in Future Urban Operations

Scott Gerwehr • Russell W. Glenn

United States Army

RAND
ARROYO CENTER

The research described in this report was sponsored by the United States Army under Contract No. DASW01-01-C-0003

Library of Congress Cataloging-in-Publication Data

Gerwehr, Scott, 1968–
    Unweaving the Web : deception and adaptation in future urban operations / Scott Gerwehr, Russell W. Glenn.
        p. cm.
    "MR-1495."
    Includes bibliographical references.
    ISBN 0-8330-3159-7
    1. Urban warfare. 2. Deception (Military science) I. Glenn, Russell W. II.Title.

U167.5.S7 G4724 2002
355.4'26—dc21

                                                            2002024930

RAND is a nonprofit institution that helps improve policy and decisionmaking through research and analysis. RAND® is a registered trademark. RAND's publications do not necessarily reflect the opinions or policies of its research sponsors.

Published 2002 by RAND
1700 Main Street, P.O. Box 2138, Santa Monica, CA 90407-2138
1200 South Hayes Street, Arlington, VA 22202-5050
201 North Craig Street, Suite 202, Pittsburgh, PA 15213
RAND URL: http://www.rand.org/
To order RAND documents or to obtain additional information, contact Distribution Services: Telephone: (310) 451-7002;
Fax: (310) 451-6915; Email: order@rand.org

PREFACE

Urban terrain is a great facilitator of deception. Combatants in any type of urban conflict (and at any level of war) can and do make effective use of deception for offensive, defensive, or intelligence-gathering purposes. Yet the *science* of deception is relatively under-developed, and numerous questions about the cost and benefit tradeoffs of employing deception remain unasked and, therefore, unanswered. The research and analysis reported here was under-taken to elaborate upon existing deception theory and propose new paths for technological, doctrinal, educational, and experimental development. The primary source for the principles and prescriptions described in this report is the voluminous literature of animal and plant biology, specifically as it relates to the practice of deception.

This study will be of interest to armed forces, law enforcement, and intelligence community personnel planning for or conducting operations and training in urban terrain. Specifically, those who face the challenge of employing or combating deception should find the contents of this report a stimulus to thinking comprehensively and innovatively about the topic. Other governmental or nongovernmental agencies considering policies involving the dedication of military, law enforcement, or intelligence assets in urban settings will likewise find material of value in generating alternate or novel approaches in applying or countering deception. Finally, the authors hope to find an interested audience in academia, particularly among those studying animal biology and behavior. We believe that a great deal of mutual benefit is to be gained when different disciplines bring their respective analysis to bear on a shared problem set.

This research was undertaken for the Assistant Secretary of the Army (Acquisition, Logistics, and Technology) and was conducted in the Force Development and Technology Program of RAND Arroyo Center. The Arroyo Center is a federally funded research and development center sponsored by the United States Army.

For more information on RAND Arroyo Center, contact the Director of Operations (telephone 310-393-0411, extension 6500; FAX 310-451-6952; e-mail donnab@rand.org), or visit the Arroyo Center's Web site at http://www.rand.org/ard/.

CONTENTS

CHARTS AND FIGURES

Charts

Figures (following page 32)

TABLES

SUMMARY

Deception is widely appreciated as a powerful instrument of war, yet it is surprisingly understudied. There is much to be learned from the flexibility and innovation demonstrated at times by opposing forces. The authors believe that this holds as true in training exercises as in actual deployments. While there is no lack of ingenuity and guile among U.S. service members (at any rank), there is little training in "how to craft and employ ruses" and relatively few resources tasked to support deception operations. The authors have also noted that there is little analysis or doctrinal guidance for combatants or commanders to mull over when making tradeoffs regarding deception, even for so simple a question as whether to employ camouflage or decoys.

This research was conducted in an attempt to delve more deeply into the theory of deception and, in so doing, to reveal new avenues of experimentation. These pathways may lead to new technologies or new training techniques, and hopefully will provoke a new look at deception doctrine applicable at every level of war. After reviewing the military deception literature, the authors examined a wide range of research on deception in the animal kingdom, where ruses of virtually infinite variety are applied to offense, defense, and intelligence gathering. What fundamentally ties animal deception to military deception? Since all entities seek accuracy in their perceptions, and accurate perceptions rely heavily upon the performance of an individual's sensors, improvements to sensors or sensory processing are significant contributors to survival; this is as true for human combatants as it is for any animal in any environment. It should not be surprising, therefore, that the reverse holds true: capabilities that engender *inaccuracy* in the perceptions of the foe (be it attacker or defender) tend to be highly advantageous. This capability is defined as *deception*, and the advantage it provides stems from the erroneous action that so often follows an inaccurate perception.

Although the literature on deception in animal biology has only recently emerged from naturalism and become an experimental science, it is richer and more scientifically rigorous than the corresponding literature on military deception. This should not be taken as a criticism of the quality of work on military deception, but rather a comment on its nature: there is relatively little *scientific* literature on military deception. What experimental work exists is often narrowly focused, and the remainder of the literature is made up of informed opinion and illustrative anecdote. In light of this, the authors have sought to mine animal biology for suggestive lessons and experimental hypotheses on deception and counterdeception. The authors found this enterprise to be of value in several respects:

Deception can be of immense value. The unforgiving nature of natural selection, combined with a truly staggering prevalence of deception, strongly supports the argument that causing an adversary's perceptions to be inaccurate (i.e., degrading their situational awareness) is of enormous value in virtually any setting or type of conflict. As an adaptation, deception techniques are as important as improvements to speed, armor, and weapons; why, then, does the U.S. military accord deception such little *actual* importance? What can be done to change this, and what can be gained thereby? More emphasis and tighter integration of deception in tactics, techniques, and procedures (TTPs) into operations and technological development would clearly be of benefit, particularly in a world of asymmetrically minded opponents.

Deception is a complex phenomenon that requires a nuanced analytic approach. There are many deceptive methods that may accomplish similar ends, and the details of the deceptions matter greatly. Some deceptions rely mainly on the physical realm, while others emphasize the behavioral realm. Some deceptions are fixed and unchanging, while others show great flexibility and may even be tailored to particular opponents. The authors have identified at least three axes along which to measure individual deceptions, and at least three means by which individual deceptions may be aggregated.

When faced with an individual deception, the warfighter or analyst can usefully distinguish between different levels of sophistication (static, dynamic, adaptive, premeditative); different effects sought (masking, misleading, confusing); and different means of deception (morphological, behavioral). Moreover, deceptions in practice are often aggregations of individual deceptions, and such aggregation can be across physical space and time, or can be synergistic combinations of individual methods. The authors found the complexities and nuances of animal deception a rich source of material in developing deception theory for both prescriptive and proscriptive ends. Moreover, this material proved to be a wellspring of numerous questions that must be asked about military deception, and it suggests experiments that may answer them with an ultimate aim of improved cost/benefit analysis of deception.

As noted in their previous work (Gerwehr and Glenn, 2000), the authors have found that synergy arises when deception is conducted in urban terrain. The characteristics of urban environments—the density of structures, the teeming population, the complexity of terrain, the multiplicity of channels for communication, the voluminous background "noise," the prodigious quantity and heterogeneity of resources—allow for a great diversity and enhanced effectiveness of deception measures. **The vast majority of deceptions practiced in the animal kingdom have valuable analogs in urban terrain.** The authors believe that from animals there are useful insights to be gained about all military deception in all environments, yet the benefits to urban operations will be greatest.

The term "adaptation" is often used when describing the learning and innovation of combatants in military conflicts, particularly in urban operations. Many of these adaptations involve improvements to deception methods, that is, means for degrading or manipulating an adversary's situational awareness. Not surprisingly, this type of adaptation is tremendously commonplace and valuable in animal biology. An observer can begin to characterize combatants along a spectrum of adaptability, a descriptor we call the *adaptive index.* Further, an analysis of this type has a prescriptive role quite apart from its descriptive one. As we consider why combatants innovate, the rate at which such innovation occurs, and with what means innovation is institutionalized, **a doctrine for countering adversary adaptation begins to emerge**. The authors believe that this type of guidance is especially needed in urban operations, where the qualities and pace of adversary adaptation have significant, even decisive, consequences. Moreover, the authors believe that U.S. forces may want to consider instituting means (in both training and technology) that encourage adaptations (devolved to the company, platoon, or squad levels) as a counterweight to those of the adversary.

Having studied deception at some length, the authors believe that although counterdeception is an important component of reconnaissance and surveillance (R&S), the two concepts are not equal. Counterdeception is a skill set of its own that requires conscious allocation of resources and training. The authors identified at least five distinct categories of counterdeception (focusing upon data type, data collection, data analysis, unmasking deception with deception, and rendering deception moot). We hypothesize that **the most effective approaches to penetrating deception entail (1) combining more than one category of counterdeception and (2) applying the right category of counterdeception.** Intelligence analysts receive counterdeception training as a distinct element in their curriculum. Given the prevalence and diversity of deceptions encountered by friendly forces in urban operations, training in counterdeception and improved counterdeception TTPs would prove quite valuable.

Adaptation features prominently in operations in urban terrain that occur or unfold over time and with multiple engagements. **U.S. forces ought to explicitly aim to interfere with or manage adversary adaptation.** Among the greatest benefits of a counteradaptive approach is in the area of counterdeception. Those adaptations that interfere with an opponent's reconnaissance and situational awareness—that is, deceptions—improve one's own survivability at the expense of the opponent. Built-up terrain supports and promotes these types of adaptations greatly. Thus, hindering an adversary's adaptation is likely to reduce the quantity and quality of deceptions that he is able to field, adding value to one's own reconnaissance efforts (and thus to every action that requires situational awareness). The authors believe that just as experiments in encouraging/improving friendly adaptation ought to be run, so should experiments and exercises in which an explicit aim of the friendly force is to hinder or otherwise manage adversary adaptation. This would be the biological equivalent of choosing from an array of selective pressures to apply to one's competitors, instead of simply leaving the choice up to chance and nature. Lessons learned on the friendly actions that are the most effective in shaping adversary adaptation would be invaluable, particularly in stability and support operations (SASO) occurring over time in urban terrain.

A better understanding of deception carries important technological implications. **As plans are drawn up for the technologies that will undergird the Interim Brigade Combat Team and Objective Force, improvements in the science of deception should figure prominently in these designs.** Given the enhanced survivability of organisms that employ well-tailored deceptions, it would appear that investment in deception science is extremely worthwhile.

ACKNOWLEDGMENTS

This document and the work it represents were made possible by the support and collaborative efforts of the entire RAND Arroyo Center urban operations team: Donna Betancourt, Lieutenant Colonel Drew O'Donnell, Sean Edwards, Paul Gaertner, Major Fred Gellert, John Matsumura, Olga Oliker, and Randy Steeb. The authors are especially grateful to Jamison Medby for her significant contributions on battlefield intelligence. Also deserving of thanks are Ken Horn and David Chu of the Arroyo Center, who provided leadership and a sure hand at the helm.

The authors have had numerous generative and stimulating discussions on deception with many people inside and outside RAND, all of whom merit thanks. We are grateful to Robert Anderson, Alisa Borden, Jennifer Brower, Gary Cecchine, Linda Demaine, Matthew Feitshans, Philip Feldman, Gene Gritton, Rich Moore, Kevin O'Connell, Bruce Pirnie, Bill Rosenau, Jeff Rothenberg, John Stillion, Alan Vick, and Robert Weissler for their efforts in advancing this research. We have also benefited greatly from the support of members of the intelligence community in conducting related research; we extend our sincerest thanks to them.

The authors also recognize the professionalism and dedication of this document's reviewers. Dr. Philip Antón of RAND and Randall (Doc) Scheffler (U.S. Army, retired) have generously offered their time and insights to improve this report. The authors also wish to thank Nikki Shacklett of RAND for her excellent editorial skills, and Priscilla Glenn for her superb art and design efforts.

ABBREVIATIONS

APC	armored personnel carrier
BDU	battle dress uniform
BLUFOR	blue force
CCD	camouflage, concealment, and deception
COA	course of action
COMINT	communications intelligence
FLIR	forward-looking infrared radar
FLN	Front de Libération Nationale
FOPEN	foliage-penetrating
GPS	global positioning system
HARM	high-speed anti-radiation missile
HQ	headquarters
HUMINT	human intelligence
IAD	integrated air defense
IFF	identification, friend or foe
IMINT	imagery intelligence
IPB	intelligence preparation of the battlefield
IR	infrared

JSEAD	joint suppression of enemy air defenses
JSTARS	joint surveillance, targeting, and reconnaissance system
LO	low observable
LTTE	Liberation Tigers of Tamil Elam
MANPADS	man-portable air defense system
MCCD	multispectral close combat decoy
NATO	North Atlantic Treaty Organization
NEO	noncombatant evacuation operation
NGO	nongovernmental organization
NIR	near infrared
OPFOR	opposing force
OPLANS	operational plans
OPTEMPO	operational tempo
PGM	precision guided munition
PIRA	Provisional Irish Republic Army
P_k	Probability of kill
ROE	rules of engagement
SAR	synthetic aperture radar
SEAD	suppression of enemy air defenses
SIGINT	signals intelligence
SOP	standard operating procedures (or standing operating procedures)
TTPs	tactics, techniques, and procedures
UAV	unmanned aerial vehicle

Chapter One

INTRODUCTION

[A]mong all these evolutionary achievements, perhaps none are more important, more widely used, and more highly developed, than those characteristics which serve to elude, to attract, or to deceive the eye, and so facilitate escape from enemies or the pursuit of prey. (Cott, 1966)

CCD [camouflage, concealment, and deception] employment increases survivability. (Joint CCD Program FY95 annual report)

What do defense planners have to learn from animal and plant biology, particularly in the area of deception? The answer is not immediately obvious, relative to what might be learned, for example, from a historical review of earlier military engagements. As defense analysts and decisionmakers grapple with the difficult challenges of operating in urban environments, animal and plant biology might seem at a far remove from obvious utility. Yet previous research (Gerwehr and Glenn, 2000) has observed a powerful resonance between military deception in urban environments and biological deception techniques—techniques that are highly effective and commonplace in support of species survival. This resonance is particularly apparent for objectives that are *proximate* rather than *ultimate*. In other words, the nexus between biological and military deception is most visible when the deception benefits the deceiver immediately and directly (*proximately*). For example, studies in animal behavior have found that camouflage is often more effective in cluttered, densely populated areas, possibly due to the greater amount of information present and the concomitant difficulty an individual organism has in tracking and sorting it. A reasonable analogy might be drawn between this finding and military operations in urban terrain, where identifying concealed combatants within a huge population of active noncombatants and complex, man-made terrain is a longstanding and formidable problem. Studies on "cognitive load" in the literature of social psychology seem to echo this point (Milgram, 1970; Cohen, 1978).

Our current effort seeks to build on that earlier work by delving more deeply into the variety of biological deceptions to distill further lessons with application in the military domain, specifically in urban operations. As such, this report represents the convergence of two lines of inquiry:

- The staggering variety of deceptions in the animal and plant kingdoms demonstrates the vital importance and ubiquity of deception in nature. Deception is simply one of the most valuable instruments of biological survival. Human deception differs from that found in other species only by degree; virtually every type of deception conducted by human beings (particularly in military affairs) is mirrored in nature (e.g., decoys, camouflage, diversions, disinformation, dazzles, disruptive coloration, disguise). All are found in the animal and plant kingdoms, and they are found not once but repeatedly throughout every environment and in species from microbes to mammals.

- Furthermore, animal and plant deception—like military deception—varies widely in its sophistication, complexity, cost, risk, and effectiveness. In the course of previous research, a thorough mining of animal and plant literature proved extremely valuable in developing a comprehensive theory of deception, one broad enough to encompass human, animal, and plant alike.

U.S. intelligence-collection assets have greater difficulty in accurately picturing the urban environment than any other; the urban setting is the most conducive to deception of any operating environment. Compared to others, the urban environment has the richest lodes of materials, the greatest background noise, the highest operational tempo (OPTEMPO), and the most complex terrain, and it also exacts the greatest toll on sensor and communication effectiveness. Moreover, urban environments have the greatest numbers of noncombatants and nongovernmental organizations (NGOs) present. This alone presents an array of challenges to situational awareness: "normal" activity is so voluminous and varied that it is difficult to notice "abnormal" activity. In time of war, of course, gauging what is "normal" baseline activity is exceedingly problematic, greatly facilitating the possibilities for deception of all sorts.

Deception thrives in this setting. A wealth of available materials increases the sophistication of deceptions; voluminous activity improves masking efforts and overloads the adversary's intelligence efforts; complex terrain creates uncertainty and diffuses vigilance; degraded sensing and communications blur the intelligence picture; and a high OPTEMPO precludes deliberate, unhurried perception and erodes decisionmaking. The possibility of conducting deception, the variety of possible deception efforts, the likelihood of deception success, and the ultimate effect of successful deception are all amplified in urban terrain relative to other terrain types.

Chapter Two

OBJECTIVES OF THIS REPORT

The authors began with this question: How exactly can a better understanding of deception in nature help prescribe deception and counterdeception measures in military matters, specifically in urban operations?

In framing an answer, we sought to accomplish two principal aims:

1. Expand and elaborate upon existing deception theory.

2. Open new avenues of experimentation for deception in both exercises and simulations.

We have an opportunity to improve on existing frameworks for classifying and comparing deceptions. This enterprise is the first step toward a genuine *science* of deception, which is necessary if we are to credibly perform cost/benefit analysis of deception options. Furthermore, theory lends itself to deduction and may be taught more readily than ad hoc approaches or ingenuity. What may work in the desert against one foe will not necessarily apply against a different foe operating within a city. Rather than placing the burden upon the unstructured creativity of individuals, a well-developed theory of deception—founded on experimentation and analysis— will be more useful as the mission, the battlefield, the equipment, and the foes change. This is not to say that the inspiration of individuals should be underrated; it is instead to assert that there is much room for doctrine to improve.

We also intend to make a fundamental point about conflict (and particularly urban conflict): evolutionary principles apply, particularly with regard to adversary *adaptation,* which we define as the process by which an individual or group becomes better fitted to its circumstances. Why make this point? If an evolutionary model *can* be said to apply, then a great deal of prescriptive value follows. Adaptations will most often take the form of variations on existing tactics or technologies, although some conditions will accelerate or diversify innovations. Such conditions could be plentiful resources, rapid generational turnover, programs of directed adaptation (i.e., research and development), a proclivity for diversifying, and so on. If beneficial adaptations are to become widespread, then time, supplies, and communications are required. During the intelligence preparation of the battlefield (IPB) process, some adversaries may be deemed more or less adaptive than others (each has an *adaptive index*). Courses of action (COAs) may be chosen accordingly. In fact, upon analysis it may turn out that some COAs are more or less likely to give rise to adversary adaptation. Furthermore, concepts of operation may dictate that elements required for successful adaptation (e.g., communications) must be explicitly denied to the adversary, specifically to prevent innovation. We will term this kind of activity *counteradaptation methodology.*

Consider how this model might apply to the overall goal of countering adversary deception, which may be described as consisting of three parts: preventing adversary deception operations; detecting and identifying adversary deceptions; and thwarting or defeating adversary deceptions. We will explore how this last component is directly related to our concept of counteradaptation, specifically in urban environments, which are the most dense in terms of quantity and heterogeneity of resources, population, and conduits of communication. Information can travel quickly in the medium of an urban environment (Edwards, 2001), and disseminated information is the vector of adaptation in military conflict. Preventing adversaries from successfully employing deception in urban operations— whether in the form of personal or vehicular disguise, false radio transmissions, feints and other diversionary activities, lures and invitations to ambush, or any other form of urban deception—would surely be of significant value.

The authors also see in the literature of animal and plant deception an opportunity to learn important lessons about urban operations generally and urban deception in particular. These are lessons that may serve as experimental hypotheses to be tested; as prescriptions for technological, doctrinal, and organizational innovation; or even simply as cautionary tales to be heeded by military decisionmakers. An important caveat: the mapping between the biological and military domains varies in its precision, and we shall strive to bear this in mind as we proceed. There is probably close to 1:1 mapping between animals, plants, and humans when it comes to camouflage based upon color, texture, and shape. Thus camouflage may be considered the high water mark of the relationship (that is, a lesson learned about effective camouflage in animals may well map *directly* into efforts to improve human camouflage). But other lessons from animal and plant biology may be more provocative than prescriptive, wherein the utility of the lesson is in stimulating creativity as opposed to simply driving design improvement. In this research, we have tried to distill what has been learned about deception in biology into axioms relevant to the urban operator.

Chapter Three

LESSONS ON DECEPTION FROM ANIMAL BIOLOGY

OVERVIEW: DRAWING LESSONS FROM NATURE

[I]t is no exaggeration to say that the modification of outward appearance by visual characteristics, directed towards a seeing public,
and serving either to facilitate recognition or to frustrate it, has been
one of the main results attained in the evolution of higher animals;
and such characteristics comprise some of the most outstanding
examples of adaptation in the whole field of biology. (Cott, 1966)

Within a particular patch of woodland, swamp, desert, or ocean, it is
common to find dozens or even hundreds of examples of deception
that vary widely in form and effectiveness. The clouded leopard seen
in Figure 1 (see following page 32) illustrates one of many forms of
camouflage coloration.

There are countless examples of camouflage, disruptive coloration,
disguises, feints and demonstrations, feigned retreats, false or misleading communications, and so on. In nature, deception is ubiquitous, overwhelmingly diverse, and spanning the length of the fossil
record (Lamont, 1967, 1969; Eldredge, 1980; Thulborn, 1994; Kacha
and Petr, 1995).

Previous work by the authors has detailed the relationship between
deception and the urban environment (Gerwehr and Glenn, 2000)
and the trouble it can present to friendly forces in urban operations;
with this new effort we hope to begin the journey from diagnosing
the problem to prescribing the solution. As described in that previous work, the authors reaped a bounty of insights on deception and
counterdeception by delving into the experimental biological litera-

ture. We specifically wish to examine these biology-based insights as hypotheses in the context of urban operations for two reasons stemming from that previous research:

- The authors detect a potent synergy between urban operations and deception. The combatant who takes to urban ground as a means of blunting his opponent's sword while sharpening his own is very likely to see deception techniques as a whetstone, if not another weapon altogether.

- The urban environment, with its dense infrastructure and diverse resources, nourishes innovation (read: adaptation) more than any other operating environment. In the case of deception, the authors contend that the urban environment can support a number and breadth of possible ruses vastly greater than in any other operating environment (for example, consider the myriad deceptive uses to which a common desktop PC and printer might be put: creating forged documents, doctoring video, sending phony e-mail, etc.).

APPLYING INSIGHTS FROM BIOLOGY TO URBAN OPERATIONS

[It] may well be a labyrinth, but it is a labyrinth forged by men, a labyrinth destined to be deciphered by men. (J.L. Borges, *Tlon, Uqbar, Orbis Tertius*)

When studying the methods by which animals and plants employ deception to attack, escape, discover, or attract, we have continually found ourselves asking: *Do the principles that govern deception use in nature apply to deception use in military conflict?* Moreover, *will identifying and applying these principles in a military setting be valuable?*

We have derived from the principles of animal and plant deception a set of insights and hypotheses that might be applied on the urban battlefield. Our goal was to accomplish both prescriptive and analytic ends: first, where we see the possibility for useful capabilities and methods that are not already in our arsenals, we map from animal biology into the military domain; second, when we wish to gain a useful analytic perspective on existing capabilities and methods, we map from the military domain into animal biology. To simply illustrate these two applications of theory:

- Since animals frequently use deception to gain valuable intelligence, that principle should at least be explored for military purposes. Some birds of prey screech in a manner that suggests they are swooping in for a kill (when they are doing nothing of the sort), and this often has the effect of causing hidden prey to break cover and run for their lives. Is there any *a priori* reason why unmanned aerial vehicles (UAVs) or precision-guided munitions (PGMs) couldn't accomplish something similar? Or at a higher level of war, consider the exercise preceding BLUE SPOON (later renamed JUST CAUSE): U.S. forces learned a great deal about the readiness, organization, and likely responses of the Panamanian Defense Forces (PDF) merely by watching them react to the U.S. exercise (McConnell, 1991; Donnelly, Roth, and Baker 1991). While the authors do not suggest that the exercise was a deception, future exercises could be (and might be designed with quite specific manipulative ends in mind). Judging from the applications of deception in the animal kingdom, a demonstration with the goal of gathering intelligence on the PDF would be an entirely apt use of deception.

- Modifications to synthetic aperture radar (SAR) which allow for improved acquisition of targets *concealed* by debris or foliage do not automatically yield improved discrimination of *decoy* versus real targets. In fact, there may actually be a penalty incurred in the latter task when acquisition sensitivity increases! Consider the case of seabirds hunting the flat periwinkle *Littorina obtusata* (a marine snail) on North Atlantic beaches. Research has demonstrated that seabirds form detailed "search images" of their prey to spot periwinkles camouflaged against bladder wracks (a type of seaweed) (Owen, 1980). This search image is a very specific template of objects and characteristics looked for when hunting, and by using this template the seabirds optimize their foraging for hidden periwinkles. Yet periwinkles are highly polymorphic, and many individual periwinkles are colored in a fashion entirely unlike the version in the birds' search image; they don't blend in, but rather stand out. To the predatory seabirds, they are well-hidden in plain sight, for the seabirds' strategy of spotting periwinkles camouflaged against bladder

wracks actually *interferes* with their ability to see these conspicu-
ous ones. The specifications are too narrow, and what doesn't
match the template is discarded. This finding is echoed else-
where in experimental animal biology, such as the work of
Pietrewicz and Kamil (1981), and it reasonably suggests that
modifications to SAR which tighten the specifications in order to
raise the signal/noise ratio or reduce the time of analysis might
be counterproductive relative to other needs.

So how do these exercises in theory help us operate better in the urban environment? Consider the principles illustrated in the seabird-
versus-periwinkle example as applied to targeting adversary vehicles
in a city. When friendly forces demonstrate the capability to detect,
identify, and destroy adversary armored personnel carriers (APCs),
an adaptive adversary will resort to vehicles and traffic patterns that
break with the "search image" in use by friendly targeteers. This
might mean using civilian vehicles, disguising military vehicles to
look like civilian vehicles, or employing military vehicles in unusual
ways (such as on civilian roadways, at civilian speeds, surrounded by
noncombatants, etc.). This is very much an evolutionary model: the
selective pressure of improved targeting results in advantageous
adaptation (deception) by the surviving targets and their "offspring,"
and this process cycles over the course of a campaign in what is
termed "coevolution" (Slatkin and Maynard Smith, 1979; Dawkins
and Krebs, 1979).

IS MILITARY DECEPTION LIKE ANIMAL DECEPTION?

A blow to the head is the most effective way of killing an animal and
many predators make their initial strike at the prey's head. Many
butterflies in the family Lycaenidae have false heads at the tips of
their hindwings well away from their true heads. The impression of
a head is given by antennae-like extensions on the tip of the hindwings. These are moved up and down after the butterfly has
alighted in the way that an insect's antennae often are, while the
real antennae are kept still. (Owen, 1980)

[I]n addition to hiding tactical assets, camouflage paint patterns can
also be used to create certain tactical advantages. An example of
this can be seen on Canadian CF-18 aircraft that carry a "false

cockpit" on the bottom—a confusing illusion that could give the pilot a fractional second advantage in some dogfight situations. (*Jane's Defence Weekly,* September 2000)

Does the word "deception" mean the same thing when describing animals as when describing military actions? Let us examine the definition of deception from the joint military literature:

> Those actions executed to deliberately mislead **relevant** decision-makers as to friendly military capabilities, intentions, and operations, thereby causing the **relevant decisionmaker** to take specific actions that will contribute to the accomplishment of the friendly mission. (*Joint Publication 3-58: Joint Doctrine for Military Deception;* amended in bold by authors in Gerwehr and Glenn, 2000)

The phrase "actions executed" is sweeping: this could refer to the production and manipulation of physical objects such as false maps, misleading behaviors such as feints, or any combination of the two. The phrase "deliberately mislead" indicates that deceiving is a purposeful action taken by one party to affect another party (the "relevant decisionmaker"); deception as defined here is neither inadvertent nor self-inflicted. The phrase "friendly military capabilities, intentions, or operations" is meant to encompass the entire spectrum of target perceptions salient to the conflict: who the combatants are, what they are doing, how and why they are doing it, where they are going and when, and so on. Finally, the joint definition points out that deception is rarely conducted for its own sake: the aim of deception is to create an advantage for the deceiver. Chart 1 illustrates the joint definition of deception.

A well-developed definition for deception in animal biology (from Mitchell, 1986) is actually quite similar upon close scrutiny:

1. An organism R registers something Y from organism S, where S can be described as benefiting when

2. R acts appropriately toward Y, because

3. Y means X to R, and

4. It is untrue that X is the case.

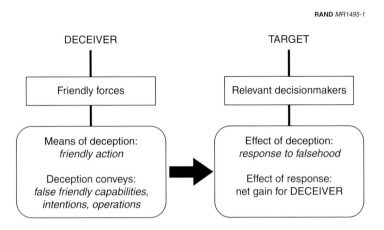

RAND *MR1495-1*

Chart 1—Deception: The Joint Definition

Simply put, the deceiver (S) employs some means (Y) against the target (R) that makes him think something false (X), which leads the target to make a mistake that the deceiver benefits by. To illustrate: The European nightjar bird (S) feigns injury (Y) to the fox (R) that is seeking the nightjar's nest, making the fox think the nightjar is an easy meal (X), whereupon the fox leaves off hunting for the nest and pursues the nightjar. After leading the fox away from the nest site, the nightjar flies away and the fox loses both bird and nest.

The term "registers" in the definition simply refers to an individual R perceiving and attending to relevant stimuli, meaning that there need not be thinking or deliberation on either side of the equation, only the transmission and reception of information. The Y term is the animal/plant equivalent to "actions executed" in the joint definition above: individual S may do, make, or employ anything Y such that R perceives and attends to it and it is relevant. The relevancy is built in by the necessity that R acts in a particular way upon receiving the transmission and S benefits by this reaction. The X term (the meaning R assigns to Y) is the equivalent of the joint definition's "friendly capabilities, intentions, and operations" and is false. Chart 2 illustrates this definition of deception used in animal biology.

RAND *MR1495-2*

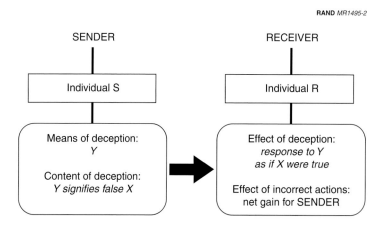

Chart 2—Deception: The Biological Definition

Although the literature on deception in animal biology has only recently emerged from naturalism and become an experimental science, it is richer and more scientifically rigorous than the corresponding literature on military deception. This should not be taken as a criticism of the quality of exposition on military deception, but rather a statement of its nature: there is relatively little *scientific* literature on military deception. What experimental work exists is often narrowly focused, and the remainder of the literature is made up of informed opinion and illustrative anecdote. Accordingly, the authors have sought to mine animal biology for suggestive lessons and experimental hypotheses on deception and counterdeception. This immediately raises an important question: To what extent is the camouflage of a spider, shark, or hawk *comparable* to the camouflage of a soldier's battle dress uniform (BDU), tank, or fighter plane? To what extent is the dangling lure of the angler fish (*Lophius piscatorius*) similar to the mannequin propped up by a Serb sniper to draw fire from enemy snipers? And we might legitimately ask the same question of the diversions, disguises, and other deception techniques seen in nature. The precise answer is unclear, but the authors hope that the following "lessons" demonstrate that animal deception and military deception are provocatively close in their methods and objectives (and by extension, in how they can be countered).

USEFUL INSIGHTS FROM ANIMAL DECEPTION

We have chosen the following three "lessons learned" because they are "unsolved" problems: that is, these are areas that the U.S. armed forces are working to improve. Moreover, they are of particular relevance to the urban environment, and we intend to provoke discussion and debate on the active motion camouflage, multiple modes of deception used in concert, and subversion/infiltration, all as applied to urban operations. While the authors do not claim that problems have been solved in all their complexity within the experimental literature of biology, we do suggest that valuable practices and observations may be gained from looking therein.

Lesson 1: Masking Signature While in Motion

> **Camouflage**: The use of natural or artificial material on personnel, objects, or tactical positions with the aim of confusing, misleading, or evading the enemy. (Joint Pub 1-02)

> Usually, the optic flow [on the surface of the retina] produced by a moving object is inconsistent with that produced by a stationary one. Evidently, the visual systems of many animals are capable of detecting this inconsistency, but this poses the question: how can one animal (or agent) track, or "shadow" another without giving itself away by its own motion . . . to [the authors'] knowledge, the problem of active motion camouflage has not been considered previously. (Srinivasan and Davey, 1995)

The utility of camouflage is very widely appreciated (Cott, 1966; Hartcup, 1979; Stanley, 1998; Owen, 1980). The rattlesnake in Figure 2 (see following page 32) demonstrates the effectiveness of camouflage coloration/patterning when matched well with the environment. From the infantryman to the joint force commander, every combatant recognizes that effective camouflage and concealment figures prominently in the formulae for survival and success. This enduring element of warfighting is just as visible in the tactics of 12th-century Saracens (Dewar, 1989) as it is in the tactics of 21st-century Serbs (U.S. Air Force Headquarters, 2000). Yet, as mentioned previously, numerous questions remain unanswered about the exact utility, parameters, variability, and longevity of camouflage. One need but look at the literature of animal biology to begin finding promising approaches to acquire those answers. Questions posed experimentally of nonhuman species that employ camouflage are strikingly similar to the questions we pose here: How much camouflage (termed crypsis in biology) is enough to provide useful protection (Pietrewicz and Kamil, 1981)? How much is too much (i.e., wasted effort)? How long can camouflage be expected to last (Dawkins, 1971)? How does its value vary over the course of time and through a series of hostile encounters? The authors believe that these experiments and outcomes can serve as initial experimental hypotheses for testing in military settings. Consider the value of such studies, as represented by answering just a few of these questions:

- Is it worth expending resources to protect a force with "masking" camouflage if the force must frequently move? Could other force-protective measures (deceptive or not) be more apt?

- When advancing on an enemy position, how exactly should a camouflaged force be moving relative to potential observers? What should their gait be? Their angle of approach? Their speed?

- What does the curve of expected returns look like when a moving force deviates from optimizing its camouflage? We might expect a precipitous drop-off, but will that depend on *how* they are deviating or on the mere fact of deviance? Can any or all concealment value be recovered? How?

Let us focus on one key question: What happens to the value of a masking camouflage scheme when the deceiver moves? Note that to begin this discussion we deliberately choose camouflage aimed at producing a "masking" effect as opposed to "confusing" or "misleading" effects. Traditionally, this common type of camouflage is seen as valuable only when it is applied to a motionless target. As far as the authors know, there is no research on the topic of what happens to the camouflage of a tank, or truck, or soldier when in motion. Presumably its value lessens, but by how much? The authors have seen little research in the military domain that investigates such questions as

- How much camouflage masking value (v) is lost given increases of motion (m) in terrain of type (t), etc.?

- Are there types of motion, or angles of movement relative to observers, or rates of speed that preserve some of the value of camouflage? Which preserve the value and by how much?

- How does the environmental context affect the value and preservation effect?

- Can the value of the camouflage be preserved by employing additional measures (colored smoke, environmental effects, ambient noise, diversions/distractions, etc.)?

- Should camouflage be designed in part for stillness and in part for motion?

and so on. As we shall discuss (see Table 1, page 30), there are a great many valuable questions about deception that are at present unanswered. The authors believe that these additional questions about camouflage and motion may be seen as *representative* of the kinds of detailed knowledge that U.S. forces should be actively seeking. It is certainly critical that experiments and exercises be conducted to directly address the issue for military purposes. The literature of animal biology is a valuable resource in this regard: we may mine it for useful questions as well as a suggestive array of answers.

If we have made the case that the literature of animal biology/deception can provoke questions, what about putative answers? If camouflage is less valuable when the subject is moving, what stratagems are animals employing to preserve or supplant that value? Consider three examples of species that have tackled the reducing-signature-while-in-motion problem in decidedly different ways. All seek an initial masking effect but with varying objectives, means, and outcome spaces.

- **Zone-tailed hawk (*Buteo albonatus*).** This predator hides in plain sight, as it were. It glides along within a group of vultures—commingling—using their presence as a mask to its own. Rodents upon which these hawks prey ignore vultures (which do not attack them); the presence of vultures in close proximity acts to reduce the signature of the hawk until it breaks from the group and swoops in for the kill. In this case, the camouflage is "designed" for motion and lasts right up until the hawk makes its attack. (Brown and Amadon, 1968)

- **Hoverfly (*Syritta pipiens*).** As male hoverflies seek a mate, they engage in a shadowing behavior that appears to preserve their camouflage. As the female moves, "the male yaws and moves laterally in such a way that it always stays on a line connecting the shadowee to the [stationary reference point]" (Srinivasan and Davey, 1995). In so doing, the image it produces upon the retina of the female remains unchanging, lending it the appearance of remaining itself stationary. This likely preserves the full value of whatever camouflage it has even while in motion, and it will last for as long as the male can maintain the appearance of immobility on the retina of the female. Note that this example from biology is consonant with our revised definition of deception: the target of the deception is not an "adversary decisionmaker," but rather a "relevant decisionmaker."

- **Okapi (*Okapia johnstoni*).** This grazer (pictured in Figure 3; see following page 32) has very typical camouflage coloration and countershading to reduce or prevent acquisition by predators. Its camouflage is decidedly less valuable as it moves, so the okapi "freezes" when danger threatens in order to acutely increase the potency of its camouflage pattern. However, natural selection has apparently decreed this to be insufficient deception given the predators in its environment, and thus the okapi has disruptive leg and hindquarters markings that seek not to mask but to confuse predators while in motion. It would therefore seem reasonable to characterize this camouflage pattern as relatively weak in motion but with a "surge" capability (the freezing behavior) and an overall short-lived viability as suggested by the disruptive marking contingency measure.

Clearly, there are many ways to skin the proverbial cat. Concealment while on the move might be gained through a number of methods; the examples noted above represent only a tiny fraction of the diverse means by which animals have addressed the problem. Who might benefit from looking more deeply into this topic? The authors believe that this is a lesson with wide applicability. Snipers and small units clearly could make use of anything that would improve their chances of remaining unobserved as they move from building to building, room to room. The intelligence provided by tactical UAVs might be multiplied considerably if they can flit about undetected. Vehicles that would come under fire when advancing down a thoroughfare in a column might be able to concentrate unmolested if they gather obliquely, from dispersal. The possibilities are many; the value added may be considerable. Parenthetically, the reverse side of the coin is equally valuable in each of the aforementioned cases: understanding how active motion camouflage is *defeated* in the animal kingdom is just as valuable a lesson for military purposes. Friendly forces would profit from improvements in their capabilities to acquire gunmen hidden among crowds and the like.

Lesson 2: Nesting Deceptions

> [E]ven a single individual may use several deceptive and defensive tricks when confronted by a predator, just as a predator may use several different ways of finding and overcoming its prey. (Owen, 1980)

A recurring motif in animals that employ deception is the concept of "nesting," or employing more than one type of deception to thwart foes (whether on offense or defense). It is noteworthy that natural selection, which is quite unforgiving of wasted effort, has produced more than one manifestation of deception in a single species, and many, many species nest deceptions. Moreover, these nested deceptions tend to be of different types. For example, it is common for species with camouflage (a masking effect) to also have a decoy structure or behavior (a misdirecting effect). Thus gecko lizards often have attractive, disposable tails in addition to camouflage; or the okapi mentioned in the section above has countershading plus disruptive hindquarters markings; or the angler fish *Lophius piscatorius* is marvelously camouflaged against the sea bottom yet also employs a worm-like lure to draw in potential prey.

Consider three examples of species that employ nested deceptions to great advantage. All three combine distinctly different deceptions within one individual.

- **Sepiola.** This squid's deceptions work most effectively *in concert*. When a predator approaches, the squid emits a cloud of ink between itself and the advancing foe. This ink cloud is shaped and colored roughly like the squid itself, presenting an attractive target. Yet rather than just allow the predator to choose between two likely targets, the squid changes color and darts away from the predator, lowering its own apparent value as a target.

- **Caterpillar of *Cerura vinula* moth.** This creature demonstrates the kitchen-sink approach to nesting deceptions. The caterpillar is camouflaged to mask its signature among the leaves where it feeds, and it also has a purplish-brown midsection that breaks up its outline. If spotted and approached, it inflates a neck color that sports two threatening eyespots in an attempt to appear like something bigger and frightening. This enlarging effect is also supported by its arching body, and the attempt at intimidation is supported by its lashing red tail. Parenthetically, the caterpillar also regurgitates an acrid-smelling goo, possesses a tenacious grip on its perch that is very difficult to dislodge, and has a slippery, hard patch behind its head (a likely strike spot for a predator). The deceptions do not *need* to work together or even with the caterpillar's other defenses; any one can succeed for a defensive victory.

- **European grayling (Hipparchia semele).** This butterfly's deceptions are staged temporally. Upon alighting, the butterfly flashes its forewings, which are adorned with eyespots to startle and flush out potential predators (the eyespots are also a likely strike point for predators). If a predator is present, the butterfly either flies away successfully or gets a bite taken out of the nonessential forewings. If there is no predator, the forewings are folded and the camouflaged hindwings are unfurled to cover the creature. It then leans over to eliminate shadow and hides out. The temporal aspect of this whole scheme is key, because the deceptions would be much less effective in any other sequence but are tremendously effective in actual practice.

What are the analogs in military operations, and why do they matter? The combination of camouflage plus decoys proved to be a vexing problem for NATO air power in Kosovo, and that difficulty would be magnified considerably were those same air strikes to be conducted in urban population centers. Or consider the wide range of Chechen deception measures employed against the Russians in the battle for Grozny: the combination of diversions plus disguises, or disinformation plus demonstration, or camouflage plus commingling with noncombatants. We would hypothesize that as the animal kingdom seems to demonstrate, the *combination* of deception measures can be synergistic. Furthermore, given the authors' earlier research (Gerwehr and Glenn, 2000), it seems likely that *combined or nested deceptions within the urban environment are more potent still.*

What does studying deception nesting in the animal kingdom provide for those considering deception in urban operations?

- First of all, it seems readily apparent that if one is conducting deception in the urban environment, employing multiple forms of deception can be worth the investment. Adversaries all too often rely upon one form of sensor or sensory analysis, and it is altogether unlikely that a single sensor will pierce two or more morphologically/behaviorally distinct deceptions. Put another way, *nesting deceptions usually trumps a single mode of counter-deception.* Moreover, even if a foe has two forms of reconnaissance—helicopters and ground troops, for example—it is in the nature of urban terrain to hamper intelligence and communications, not to mention making a very unwelcome venue for aviation assets. The city hinders counterdeception of many sorts (particularly those that are technologically based and those of the "outsider" or foreign force). *Confusion, ambiguous intelligence, and a high OPTEMPO—hallmarks of urban operations— are ideal deception facilitators.*

- Second, the reverse is true: more than one mode of perception must be employed, which is likely to be well worth the investment. Had Operation Allied Force adhered to applicable ground-force doctrine instead of relying exclusively upon airborne assets, the authors deem it highly likely that the effectiveness of Serb camouflage and decoy targets would have been significantly reduced if not negated. Why? Because the features of camouflage or decoys that deceive the eye at three or four miles altitude are less effective against the eye on the ground. Making camouflage or decoys equally useful against both sets of observers requires more time, more resources, and more skill. The burden upon the deceiver is therefore much greater and the execution that much more difficult.

Lesson 3: Infiltrating and Subverting

Infiltration: 1. The movement through or into hostile territory occupied by either friendly or enemy troops or organizations. The movement is made, either by small groups or by individuals, at extended or irregular intervals. When used in connection with the enemy, it infers that contact is avoided. 2. In intelligence usage, placing an agent or other person in a target area in hostile territory. Usually involves crossing a frontier or other guarded line. Methods of infiltration are: black (clandestine); grey (through legal crossing point but under false documentation); white (legal). (Joint Pub 1-02)

In deceiving the enemy as to his methods and intentions the guerrilla will use many ruses . . . *[He must have] agents working among the civilian population. (Handbook for Volunteers of the Irish Republican Army*, 1956 edition, emphasis added)

Urban zones are often densely populated with noncombatants, and among the most intractable of challenges in urban operations is the task of acquiring, identifying, engaging, and neutralizing adversary elements while they circulate among that civilian populace. Combatants with links to the local population in an urban conflict enjoy a tremendous advantage in intelligence gathering; communications networks; freedom of movement; anonymity and concealment; and availability of food, fuel, ammunition, medical treatment, and other vital resources. Combatants who are perceived as foreign bodies (or worse yet, *hostile* foreign bodies) in the corpus of the city suffer the opposite set of consequences: their senses are dulled; their communications are degraded or made more fragile; their actions are clumsy and exposed; and their logistics and resupply are more difficult. Given the disparity between these two states, it is an obvious priority for individual or small-unit urban operators to develop effective techniques for penetrating, co-opting, and installing themselves in population centers. Numerous historical examples shed light on how this might be accomplished on a large scale; useful insights may be gained from individuals' memoirs of the Provisional Irish Republican Army (PIRA) in Ireland, Irgun in Palestine, Front de Libération Nationale (FLN) in Algeria, Tamil Tigers in Sri Lanka, Hezbollah in Lebanon, Baader-Meinhof in West Germany, Chechens in Grozny, Tupamaros in Uruguay, Red Brigades in Italy, and so on.

However, the vast majority of this documentation takes the form of anecdote or informed opinion: it is useful and interesting, but not leavened to the status of testable hypotheses on infiltration and subversion.

The authors suggest that, akin to the preceding discussion of camouflage, many aspects of infiltration remain unbounded, unquantified, and therefore not fully understood. The following list represents just a few important questions on this topic for which there are currently no experimentally derived answers:

- What is the right number of individuals to attempt grey infiltration in a given scenario? Should one agent at a time be inserted, or is there strength in numbers?

- Is appearance more or less convincing than manner? Is false paperwork more or less persuasive than a seamless contextual facilitator (e.g., the target's expectations of time, place, and action are met)? How do these elements interact synergistically to create a more or less convincing deception?

- How much is black infiltration aided by masking? By misdirection? By confusion?

- What is the relationship of time to infiltration? How rapidly and at what rate should attempts be made?

- How much does desensitization (i.e., "crying wolf") help infiltration attempts? How much does disinformation (e.g., false news reports) help?

Clearly, many more such questions may be asked and experiments can and should be conducted in the military domain to arrive at answers. However, the authors are once again struck by the analogy between infiltration as seen in biology (from viruses to vertebrates) and the phenomenon as it is described above. We are not answering these questions here; instead we are proposing that biology represents a useful source of insight and method. The biological literature is replete with examples of species that infiltrate others' nests or territory to predate, escape predation, scavenge more easily, or otherwise gain advantage. Consider four examples of such species.

- **Rove beetle** (*Atemeles*). This beetle demonstrates the power of deceptive communication. It looks nothing like an ant, nor does its larva. However, the beetle's secretions calm aggressive ants and then stimulate adoptive behavior from them. Once carried into the nest, the beetle lays its eggs and the hatching larva emit a third secretion, which forces receiving ants to feed them (Holldobler, 1971). The key ingredient to this infiltration scheme is the overriding power of ant communication methods. When a seemingly legitimate order is received, the order is obeyed regardless of the unusual nature of the request. In human terms, this might be seen as exploiting high degrees of automation: passwords are among the most anemic of security systems, yet they remain among the principal means of safeguarding information systems and communications.

- **Cuckoo bird** (*Cuculus canorus*). These parasites specialize: individual female cuckoos select nests of a particular host and, when the parent is away, lay an egg of approximately the same coloration as the host's (Figure 4; see following page 32). Thus a reed-warbler specialist lays greenish, spotted eggs, whereas a redstart specialist lays pure blue eggs. The infiltration is "fire-and-forget": once the subversive egg is laid (which takes mere seconds), the female cuckoo abandons it completely. The deception relies upon the inflexible machinery of the host bird's rearing behaviors. If an egg of approximately the right form hatches in the nest, what emerges must be reared. This form of deception entirely relies on precise, prior intelligence of the target; there is no fine-tuning after the ruse is begun.

- **Marine fluke** (*Monogean trematode*). These marine parasites offer an alternative to the cuckoo model of parasitism. When these organisms attach themselves to a target fish, they draw tissue samples from the specific portion of the target to which they are anchored. They then use this material to render themselves of a texture and color that matches the location. When mutualist organisms that clean the parasites from hosts come along, the flukes are left unmolested as they appear to be part of the host. This model of infiltration might therefore be considered both more flexible and more risky than the cuckoo's. There is a wider target range (the attachment of the fluke can take place in a variety of locales on the host), but more investment and time are required.

- **Wasp mimics.** Certainly not all infiltration attempts are for offensive ends; a wide variety of insects (and spiders) mimic the common *Vespula* wasp and live alongside it. The wasp's reputation for delivering a nasty sting is well known, allowing other species that might otherwise be easy pickings for local predators to operate with some impunity. The key to this form of infiltration is using deception (mimicry) to resemble a very specific and respected member of the community whose status allows for freedoms not given to other residents. Relating this to the human realm, one immediately thinks of assuming the identity of a Red Cross worker, journalist for a well-known news organization, or cleric as opposed to just another disenfranchised citizen.

As suggested by the preceding examples, infiltration can come in a variety of forms: parasitic, where the intruder battens off of the host population without intending to kill it, or predatory, where the intruder gains ingress and sets about attempting to eradicate (consume) the host population. When the PIRA intimidates or metes out punishments (e.g., kneecapping) to the Irish Catholic population, it is assuming a parasitic role (the victims and witnesses are deliberately left alive to capitulate). On the other hand, when operatives of Hamas or the Liberation Tigers of Tamil Elam (LTTE) engage in a suicide bombing, their goal is the destruction or removal of their adversaries. Why point out this difference? Because the measures U.S. forces might take to rid a population of a parasite are necessarily different from those taken to combat a predator.

Chapter Four

A FRAMEWORK FOR DECEPTION ANALYSIS

The United States Armed Forces must establish integrated CCD [camouflage, concealment, and deception] training procedures for defenders, attackers, and intelligence personnel.
(Recommendation from Joint CCD Program FY95 Annual Report)

Consider the battle for Grozny in January 1995. Earlier work by the authors described the broad range of deception measures employed by the Chechen fighters against better-armed, numerically superior Russian forces in Grozny (Gerwehr and Glenn, 2000; examples drawn from Thomas, 1997; Lieven, 1998; Gall and De Waal, 1998; among others). For example,

- Chechens and Muslim volunteers disguised themselves and vehicles as Russian.

- Chechens and Ukrainians disguised themselves and vehicles as Red Cross.

- Chechen fighters purposefully commingled with noncombatants to close with or escape from Russian forces.

- Chechens camouflaged firing points, staging areas, command posts, and observation posts.

- Chechen decoys drew fire.

- Chechen dummies and disinformation confounded Russian intelligence analysts.

- Chechen disinformation misled Russian order of battle and COA estimates (e.g., about man-portable air defense systems).

- Chechens used feints and demonstrations to draw out hidden Russian forces.

- Chechens used false radio transmissions to give Russian units orders or create uncertainties.

- Chechens used fire and rapid maneuver (shoot-and-scoot) to disorient Russian units.

The Chechen-Russian conflict illustrates some important issues regarding deception, both what is known and what remains unknown about deception effects.

First of all, deception was effectively used for all kinds of objectives: force multiplication, force protection, and intelligence collection. Further, the breadth and depth of techniques used indicate that the Chechens were placing a great deal of emphasis on deception and doing so with both forethought and adaptability.

Second, deception was used to achieve a variety of *effects* (masking, misleading, confusing) with a variety of *means* (disguise, decoys, camouflage, feints, etc.), suggesting that Russian intelligence assets were having to wage a continuous and difficult effort to visualize the battlefield accurately, with penalties incurred for any and every intelligence shortfall (whether in acquisition, identification, or uncertainty resolution). Moreover, supporting such a broad array of methods and effects requires resources—radios, uniforms, fuel, camouflaging materials, training, planning, active management, etc.—which again highlights the proposition that the Chechens felt deception to be a critical effort. Importantly, it underlines the failure of Russian interdiction.

Third, there is very little existing capability to model or perform cost-benefit analysis of the deceptions employed. All parties would agree that deception use was instrumental in Chechen successes, but no one has determined which techniques contributed the most, how their conduct was amplified or impeded by environmental or target variables, how much was gained versus how much was invested, etc.

This chapter begins to address the third point: a more nuanced and finely resolved view of deception is the first step toward an analytic taxonomy.

TOWARD A BETTER UNDERSTANDING OF DECEPTION

Deception is an integral part of conflict and always has been. This is nowhere more true than in urban settings, where the complexity of the terrain and the density of available resources allow for a well-stocked bag of tricks. But despite its widespread use, how much is actually known about deception? Surprisingly, there is far less research and guidance than is merited. Consider the following scene:

> The commander of a tank platoon wishes to protect his unit, which is deployed to seize and hold an area of key urban terrain. Many hasty defensive measures are possible, but let us suppose time, mission, and resources permit only a few steps to be taken before the likely counterattack. Some possibilities include clear-cutting what vegetation might exist in the built-up area, emplacing obstacles, and preparing firing positions with sandbags. Among the possibilities for deceptive measures are two staples: decoys and camouflage. With regard to the likely risks and dividends of employing such deceptive measures, there are numerous important questions facing the commander, a sampling of which are shown in Table 1.

To the authors' surprise, there are not well-developed answers to these questions in doctrinal publications on military deception, and there are too many such unanswered questions. This assertion applies not only to adversary use of deception, but friendly applications of deception as well. This is *not* to say that there is any lack of appreciation for the importance of deception in the military community! From the rifleman whose life depends upon the quality of his camouflage to the general whose battle plan hinges upon the success of a feint, combatants readily agree that deception is important if not *essential* to military success. Further, we recognize that there is no lack of wily and creative tacticians in the U.S. armed forces, at all levels. But how can deception be quantified, measured, analyzed, and, ultimately, writ in doctrine with the specificity of a scientific discipline? What guidance can be provided to the soldier or marine—to combatant and commander alike—that will give them more options, better options, and improved estimates of outcome when using deception? The authors believe that well-developed deception theory is necessary; it would provide soldiers and marines useful guidance and prescriptions for deception and counterdeception to *supplement* their own ingenuity and cunning.

Table 1

Sample Questions on Employing Deception

Which deception is best?	Which is better protection for a tank: camouflage or decoys? Is the value of employing both equivalent to (camouflage plus decoys) or (camouflage multiplied by decoys) or something else?
Against whom?	Is this equally true applied against both airborne and ground enemies? Who among the enemy should be targeted? Who among the noncombatant population?
With what parameters?	Does this hold true for more than one tank? Is there an upper numeric limit on the force to be protected? How many decoys provide the right ratio of fake to real? How much is lost by missing the optimization point?
Under what conditions?	Does this answer vary by terrain type within the urban area? By lighting level? By season?
How much deliberation is required?	How carefully should decoys be emplaced? How exposed should they be to adversary reconnaissance? How much is gained (or lost) as increasing time and effort is spent on emplacement?
What is the timeframe?	How long can the camouflage be considered viable? What about camouflage for the decoys?
When is the deception unmasked?	Are camouflage or decoys rendered moot if noncombatants pass close to the site (providing a source of HUMINT to the adversary)?
What value is lost when the deception is unmasked?	Do both camouflage and decoys decrease in value by the same amount when an adversary becomes aware of their use on the battlefield? Can value be regained if the camouflage or decoys are redeployed at another location? How much value? Is there value in replacing the decoys with actual systems at some point in time (e.g., after they are determined to be fakes by the adversary)?

Among the first benefits in developing a deception theory is the generation of *measures of effectiveness*. Existing measures of effectiveness are poorly developed with regard to deception—as opposed to those for vehicle armor or protective vests, for example. Armor provides readily accessible measures of effectiveness: the ability to turn a blow, encumbrance, cost, and so on. But deception is a more difficult nut to crack: if deception persuades a little, is that worse than if

it persuades a lot? Or does it depend on the duration of the misperception it creates? Or on the degree of erroneous action it engen-
ders? A significant fraction of this research was devoted to mining
the literature of biology in order to address these questions. We
sought to develop a framework for typing, comparing, and assessing
deceptions in the hopes of applying such metrics to the military domain.

One of the first steps toward a deeper understanding of deception is
to take a more nuanced approach to the phenomenon. It is not
enough to simply note that an adversary is employing camouflage,
concealment, and deception (CCD) measures. Such an observation
is lacking in specificity and therefore equally lacking in prescriptive
value. Why? Because deception is a broad category that encom-
passes starkly different activities. For example, camouflage and decoys seek to produce very different effects upon the target's decisionmaking process and present the target with different problems to
solve. Moreover, even two techniques with the same name may be
significantly different in their level of sophistication and thus present
very different problems for the target to solve.

THREE PERSPECTIVES ON DECEPTION

Level of Sophistication

Let us consider camouflage as a representative category of deceptions. To state that an adversary's vehicles or personnel are camouflaged is only to scratch the surface of the deception. What is the
nature of the camouflage? How much consideration of defense versus offense is included in the camouflage's design? Is the camouflage
unchanging, without sensitivity to changes in the environment (light,
smoke, temperature, etc.)? Is the camouflage crafted in light of the
deceiver's experience in employing it? Is it tailored to the target's
perceptual structures and tactics for maximum effectiveness? Is it
designed to foil a broad array of observers, or just one opponent? Is
it applied to the visual spectrum alone, or does it include other por-
tions of the electromagnetic spectrum? Is it aimed at ground observers, airborne observers, or both? These are obviously just a few
of the questions that might be asked to uncover the details of a particular deception. The most important answer: camouflage (or any

other category of deception) is one in a spectrum of deceptive measures lumped together under one heading, and they may vary widely
in their effectiveness. Why? Because the details matter greatly.
Studies of deception in other fields—particularly animal biology—
suggest that environmental effects, OPTEMPO, recent history, preconceptions, warning, and a host of other factors weigh heavily in the
net effect of any deception.

Consider a simple illustration of this point: two sniper firing positions, both of which may be considered *camouflaged* but which differ
remarkably in their details (and probably their effectiveness).

- One occupies a rubbled building and has nearby debris piled up
  around it to prevent visual acquisition by enemy infantry (the
  primary target of the sniper).

- The other camouflage scheme is selected with specific attention
  to the context, the sensor capabilities, and the search strategy of
  the adversary. It also occupies a rubbled building, and similarly
  makes use of handy debris. The position and angle of firing is
  chosen to best suit the opponent's avenue of approach, while the
  exact color and shading of the netting/debris suit the lighting
  level of the area. Moreover, the position is draped in a netting
  that mimics the near-infrared (NIR) spectral reflectance of urban
  materials and a thermal blanket to dampen heat signature. This
  netting is employed in response to intelligence that places infrared imaging and radar in the hands of the opponent, and this
  camouflage might be aimed at ground troops *and* airborne reconnaissance, accounting for the presence of helicopters or
  UAVs in the arsenals of the foe. Perhaps the area around the
  firing position is also prepared to dampen muzzle-flash and
  backblast from weapons the sniper is likely to employ.

When we discuss the degree to which any particular deception attends to the adversary's sensors and preconceptions, environmental
and contextual effects, and the myriad other factors that influence
deception success or failure, we call this the *level of sophistication* of
that particular deception. Note that this phrase is intended as a
diagnostic, not a value judgment. An "unsophisticated" knife can kill
just as readily as a "sophisticated" precision-guided munition (PGM);
the utility of the diagnostic lies in its ability to more finely resolve the

Getty Images

Figure 1—The Clouded Leopard's Camouflage Is Well Suited to Its
Environment

Frank & Joyce Burek/Getty Images

Figure 2—The Western Diamondback Rattlesnake Conceals Itself Amid
Leaves and Undergrowth

Getty Images

Mike Jones; Frank Lane Picture Agency/Corbis

Figure 3—The Okapi Has Camouflaged Coloration and Disruptive Hindquarters Markings

Figure 4—The Cuckoo Egg Matches the Host Eggs Enough to Pass the Critical Tests

Photo courtesy of BRUCE COLEMAN INC., Photographer Tony Deane

Figure 5—The Blacksmith Plover Has Coloration That Disrupts Its Outline

Figure 6—An Octopus Uses One from Its Array of Possible Colors and Textures to Blend in with Its Background

Figure 7—The Serbs Used This Decoy Against NATO Forces in Kosovo, 1999

Figure 8—The Flatfish
Masks Its Presence

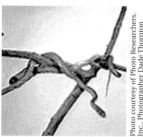

Figure 10—The
Deadly Boomslang
Appears To Be a Tree
Branch to the
Unwary

Figure 9—Amphipod Hyperiella Dilatata
Misleads Audiences with a Living Disguise

deception phenomenon and therefore lead to more precise use and countermeasures.

The level of sophistication that might characterize any given deception is a spectrum ranging from static and context-insensitive to tailored and premeditated. We can place milestones along this spectrum for the purposes of producing a more nuanced view of deception so long as these markers do not eclipse the fact that this is indeed a spectrum. The authors assert that level of sophistication progresses as Static → Dynamic → Adaptive → Premeditative, as described below.

Static deceptions are in place regardless of state, activity, or the histories of either the deceiver or target.

The standard-issue woodland BDU falls into this category; while employed in woods or jungle, it has also been worn in the desert, city, or at sea, and there is no doctrinal instruction that allows soldiers, marines, or other service members to tailor the BDU in beneficial ways.

The blacksmith plover (Figure 5; see following page 32) has disruptive coloration that can interfere with the targeting of would-be predators (note that this application of deception doesn't prevent detection, but rather the subsequent attack). While the plover's markings are generally effective in its habitat, it has no ability to turn on or off the coloring scheme nor to tune it to the particular lighting or weather conditions it finds itself in.

Dynamic deceptions are those that activate under specific circumstances. The ruse itself and the trigger do not change over time, nor do they vary much by circumstance or adversary.

The preplanned "swarm drill," whose purpose is to mask the insertion of a sniper team upon entering a building. A group of marines (including the sniper team) will overtly enter a building in relatively large numbers, assuming that they are being observed. Upon exiting and moving on, they leave behind the sniper team, and only a precise entry/egress count by an observant foe would detect the difference. Given that the marines enter and exit through multiple points in the building, an exact head count would be very difficult to accomplish.

Octopi (Figure 6; see following page 32) and squid are widely appreciated for their well-stocked inventory of deceptions. Octopi bodies contain special cells (chromatophores) that can expand and contract to manipulate their pigmentation. The function of these cells allows the octopus to appear any combination of red, orange, green, blue, brown, or even whitish. As the background changes, the octopus selects the right concealing color. To complement this capability, the octopus' mantle can also change texture: matching coral, sand, rock, or seaweed as appropriate. Why does this extraordinary complement of ruses come under the heading of dynamic, and not something higher? Because the ruses themselves do not change over time, and neither do the triggering mechanisms (i.e., changes in nearby terrain). The rules are set ahead of time (the animal equivalent of preplanning) and set in stone, even if the color parameter is continuous. This is "scenario-based" deception planning. We note that *possessing great quantities of a capability does not necessarily mean greater flexibility with regard to that capability.*

Adaptive deceptions are triggered like dynamic deceptions, but either the trigger or the ruse itself can be modified with experience. This category covers deception improved through trial and error.

An illustration of adaptive deception in an urban setting:

> [Chechen] mortars mounted on Kamaz trucks fire one salvo and immediately move to another area. They have skillfully *learned* to disorient fire spotters, often creating a friendly fire situation. Thus on the eve of the taking of the palace, a Russian Grad multiple rocket launcher fired on its own reconnaissance company in the airport region, which is ringed by mountains and forests. (Vinogradov, 1995; emphasis added)

The larvae of the green lacewing (*Chrysopa slossonae*) feed rapaciously on woolly alder aphids (*Paraprociphilus tessellatus*), stalking and killing them despite the presence of vigilant black carpenter ants that protect aphids. The lacewing larvae transfer woolly wax from the aphids' bodies to their own as they prey upon them, quickly developing a disguise that the guardian ants cannot penetrate. The reason why this form of deception is called *adaptive* as opposed to *dynamic* is that the parameters of the disguise are not fully deployed and optimized ahead of time, but are instead determined through interaction with the adversary and environment. This is more "capabilities-based" deception planning, and the set of possible deceptions produced is—if not infinite—likely to be larger and *more tailored to the precise circumstances* than under "scenario-based" planning.

Premeditative deceptions are designed and implemented based on experience, knowledge of friendly capabilities and vulnerabilities, and, moreover, observations about the target's sensors and search strategies.

The "stealth" coatings on low-observable aircraft are good examples of premeditation in deception: they are very specifically designed to thwart the radars of known (and potential) adversaries, with a specific mission (e.g., suppression of enemy air defenses) in mind and thus specific kinds of vulnerabilities to protect.

Primates, cetaceans (whales and dolphins), and humans hold the monopoly on highly sophisticated deceptions. The decoy pictured in Figure 7 (an unclassified photo taken at the Nellis AFB Threat Training Facility; see following page 32) was used by Serb forces against U.S. pilots in Operation Allied Force in 1999. Though crude—constructed of milk crates, baling wire, and green spray paint—it is a good representative of premeditative deceptions. Moreover, despite its primitive design, it drew at least a dozen strikes from Allied forces over several sorties; each time it was destroyed, Serb forces re-wrapped it, repainted it, and set it out again to draw fire on the next sortie.

The authors encountered an example of tailored, precisely targeted deception conducted by an Atlantic bottle-nosed dolphin in a May 2000 visit to the Marine Mammal Systems program in San Diego. A certain dolphin in the pod would venture out with her handler to conduct sector-by-sector mine search training. Each search in the exercise normally took a well-established length of time, after which the dolphin would return to the handler and signal whether she had encountered ordnance (training mine of the moored or buried varieties) or nothing in that sector. The handlers began to notice that this dolphin (who was healthy, but quite advanced in age) was missing training mines in her searches and considered the possibility that she might be losing some echolocation capabilities, or processing skills, or the like. However, upon investigating, they discovered that the crafty dolphin would receive her instructions and dive off as though on a search, but actually circled round and hovered underneath the handler's boat. She waited for a length of time precisely suited to the volume of water she was supposed to be searching and then resurfaced, signaling "all clear." Her assessment of the handler's expectations, manipulation of the signals, and devising of a ruse that matched the circumstances are all hallmarks of a sophisticated deception.

In application, considering the level of sophistication of particular deceptions can make valuable contributions. For example, if an urban insurgency is disguising its fighters as noncombatants, it would behoove the constabulary force to carefully consider the level of sophistication of such disguises. Hasty, poorly resourced disguises might be uncovered by simple checkpoints, while those with expertly-forged documents and ample preparation time might require chemical sniffers, a gauntlet of interviews, or other more elaborate counterdeception techniques.

Effect Sought

While the sophistication of any deception method is pivotal to its success or failure, another vital component is the type of *effect* the deception seeks to produce. By "effect" we mean the specific type of disadvantageous misperception the deceiver is seeking to produce in the mind of the target. Consider: camouflage and concealment are closely related, yet they have almost nothing in common with decoys or feints. Camouflage and concealment are *masking* techniques that reduce signals (ideally, to the point of undetectability). A warfighter or analyst seeking to overcome masking techniques is seeking to *acquire* a target in the face of opposition. But in the case of the decoy or feint, acquisition is a given; it is *identification* or discrimination that is sought. These are *misdirecting* techniques whose purpose is the clear and unambiguous transmission of a *false* signal (often in the hopes of diverting attention, resources, or attacks away from real assets or activities). The warfighter or analyst faced with misdirecting techniques must refine his or her capabilities for discerning true from false—an enterprise entirely separate from improving acquisition. A third category of methods—which the authors will term *con-*

fusing techniques—represents still another set of problems to the warfighter and analyst. These methods seek to degrade or paralyze the target's perceptual capabilities through voluminous background noise, oversaturation, unpredictability, and the need for haste. Confusing methods often interfere with *both* acquisition and identification; combating them requires a set of potential solutions to be explored quite apart from those previously mentioned. Table 2 illustrates how common CCD and other deceptive techniques map into these three major categories.

What is the defeat to be inflicted upon the target? Is the deceiver attempting to *mask* his/her signature? Is the deceiver attempting to present a signature with some element of falsity in order to *misdirect* the target to inappropriate belief? Is the deceiver seeking to *confuse* the target with paralyzing uncertainty? These are the three general types of effects sought by deception; they broadly group the type of misperception being induced by the deceiver. This is enormously

Table 2

Major Types of Deceptive Effect Sought

Deceptive Effect	Definition	Common Examples
Masking	Concealing signal	Camouflage Concealment Commingling with noncombatants Signature reduction
Misdirecting	Transmitting clear and unambiguous *false* signal	Feint/demonstration Decoy/dummy Disguise Disinformation (e.g., forged documents)
Confusing	Raising the "noise" level to create uncertainty, paralysis	Generating additional commo traffic, movement, etc. Shoot-and-scoot to disorient foes Purposeful departure from established pattern (also called conditioning/exploit) Randomization

important when we consider the information processing and decisionmaking of the target. The mental process of acquiring is quite different from the mental process of identifying, and both are different from the process of resolving uncertainty.

Consider the individual infantryman engaged in peacekeeping (patrolling) duties. If a curfew is in effect, merely *spotting* anyone moving about comprises a violation. The exact identity of that person is of minimal relevance. On the other hand, if the peacekeeper is seeking to apprehend wanted criminals, then spotting is subsidiary to *recognizing* the individual. Lastly, if our peacekeeper runs across groups of persons who appear furtive or up to no good, then, although spotting and recognizing play a role, the peacekeeper must *choose* or resolve between several different plausible explanations (and thus courses of action). Figures 8 and 9 (see following page 32) show examples of masking, misleading, and confusing techniques in the animal kingdom.

An example of a living disguise in military affairs can be seen in the accounts of U.S. Marines in Beirut, described by Hammel (1985, p. 154):

> Women were sent into the streets to reconnoiter the Marine and LAF [Lebanese armed forces] positions. The most blatant of the scouts was a heavyset middle-aged woman—or a large man dressed in a woman's clothing—who made trip after trip across the end of the alley. One of the Marine riflemen reached the end of his tether late in the afternoon and dropped her in her tracks with one M16 round. An Amal gunman who was duck-walking in the woman's ample hidden side scuttled for a nearby building when his cover fell to the street.

In application, explicit consideration of effect sought is of immediate value in planning friendly deceptions as well as countering adversary deceptions.

- Let us consider first a simple illustration on the friendly side. If U.S. or allied troops are to be deployed in a constabulary role into an urban area with great numbers of neutral or hostile noncombatants, deceptions that seek to *mask* the friendly presence are likely to be of limited utility (due to human intelligence (HUMINT), etc.). This suggests that resources like camouflaged

BDUs and netting are probably of limited value and should be deemphasized. But deceptions that seek to *mislead* should be greatly effective in the noisy, chaotic, densely populated setting of the urban landscape, and thus resources like smoke, decoys, and false radio transmission capability should be pushed up the requirement ladder.

- Now let us think about the adversary. Consider a foe who is exploiting the presence of noncombatants by deliberately introducing "false positives" into U.S. intelligence-collection efforts: staging sniping or bombing incidents, transmitting phony signals intelligence (SIGINT), passing false HUMINT rumors, etc. The effects sought are *misleading* and *confusing*. In employing them the adversary wishes to lead friendly intelligence capabilities into a labyrinth of false trails, dead ends, and wasted efforts. Recognizing that an adversary is attempting these effects instead of masking should drive numerous friendly adaptations: a greater quantity of similar surveillance probably offers little value added, but a diversification of surveillance methods is likely to offer much. Mounting additional sensors (e.g., cameras) on lampposts or low-flying UAVs offers additional *detection* capabilities and thus merely gives the adversary another opportunity to generate a false positive. Mounting different sensors (e.g., explosives sniffers) offers the ability to *discriminate* among detections and thus is the proper countermeasure to misleading-type deceptions.

Means of Deception

We have already discussed a broad definition for deception that allows for consideration of many techniques to be brought to bear against many targets (whether combatant or noncombatant) in support of the friendly mission. Whether the effect sought by a particular technique is masking, misdirecting, or confusing, the *means* by which the deception is conducted can generally be thought of as comprising two parts: the *form* and the *function*. The part that is primarily a matter of substance or form (debris, dyes, temperature, shape, etc.) is called *morphological*. The part that is primarily a matter of implementation or function (timing, location, pattern, etc.) we term *behavioral*. Thus we would say that a tank with a coat of nonreflective paint matched to its environment (in order to avoid detection) is employing a predominantly morphological deception, but a tank driving at civilian speeds on civilian roads among civilian vehicles (in order to avoid detection) is employing a deception of the behavioral type. Note that the categorization of form and function is not meant to straitjacket: some deception techniques will have elements of both. For the purposes of analyzing examples, however, we will generally assert that any individual deception has a *primary* means of achieving its effect. Thus, while an F-117's ability to remain undetected relies to some extent on pilot skill, it is to a greater extent a function of the aircraft's shape and composition.

Why should we pay attention to the different means of deception? The answer is fairly obvious: if we want to conduct deception effectively, we should have the resources to support the effort, and this includes not just physical resources (for morphologic means), but the proper training and doctrine to conduct behavioral deceptions as well.

Sophistication, Effect, and Means: The Details Matter

In the preceding sections we have attempted to offer a more finely resolved view of deception; the authors believe that dimensions of analysis are necessary to usefully bound the deception "space." Military deception and animal/plant deceptions can be understood within the same theoretic framework, and it is useful to compare one domain with the other to develop both a comprehensive view of deception and a sensitivity to important nuances that affect deception success and effect.

Categorizing deceptive techniques and behaviors is an important step toward a complete taxonomy, but it is only a first step. The ultimate goal of our research will be to fully inform decisionmakers on the topic of deception, particularly in urban operations. To proceed toward a comprehensive and useful analytic framework, we must relate deceptions of quite different sorts applied against different targets in different circumstances. The theory we hope ultimately to establish will enable decisionmakers to:

- Evaluate the costs and expected dividends from a given deception measure employed in a particular context.

- Compare the costs and benefits of any two or more deception measures, including different implementations of the same type (i.e., a range of potential investment levels in the same camouflage technique will produce a corresponding range of potential benefits).

- Make tradeoffs between the investment in deception and the investment in other friendly measures (e.g., speed, lethality, armor, intelligence collection).

- Understand the interaction between deception measures and other friendly measures (e.g., camouflage and armor, or decoys and speed, or disinformation and intelligence collection).

- Understand what type of problem is posed by different types of adversary deception measure; this will prescribe a more precise method of counterdeception.

- Perform cost and benefit analysis on candidate counterdeception measures given the range of deception(s) they face and context they are fielded in.

AGGREGATING DECEPTIONS FOR GREATER EFFECT

We have identified a minimum of four ways in which individual deceptions may be aggregated to achieve operational/strategic-level benefits:

		Application	
		Space	Time
Method	Same		
	Different		

Individual deceptions can vary in their method and, moreover, in where and when they are applied.

- **Employing multiple, similar methods of deception.** Individual ruses can be employed en masse. For example, decoys can obviously be used one at a time or in groups.

- **Employing multiple, different methods of deception.** Ruses may differ in form, may be aimed at different targets, and may induce different (though complementary) misperceptions. For example, a false map purporting to depict a belt of obstacles and strong points in a city, placed into the hands of an enemy patroller, along with a demonstration by armored vehicles and infantry, both communicate a false impression of defender tactics, techniques, and procedures (TTPs) to enemy reconnaissance. False radio messages could likewise misrepresent the location and vulnerability of critical nodes in the city to enemy SIGINT while, further, members of the indigenous population pretending to be sympathetic to the enemy cause communicate false vulnerabilities. Who falls prey to these deceptions individually/tactically may incur negative operational or strategic consequences.

- **Applying deception at different points in time.** Individual deceptions may occur in a sequence devised to engender operational or strategic effects. Consider this simple illustration: What occurs in the mind of an infantryman "hunkered down" in the rubble if what starts out as the sounds of distant, sporadic gunfire becomes a torrent of shots (perhaps interspersed with explosions) nearby? An individual ruse (staged sniper fire) can be employed with others (of a kind, or different) *over time* to create desired effects. In this simple case, it may be that headquarters (HQ) begins receiving reports of an impending attack.

- **Applying deception at different points in space.** Deceptions conducted at different places may have a synergistic effect. In a simple illustration of this point, consider the combatant whose reconnaissance elements spot enemy forces (actually dummies) in each of the cardinal directions. Such a combatant may conclude that he or she is surrounded and take appropriate action: shifting from offensive to defensive postures, or even surrendering (in the most extreme case). Although this is a simple example, it nevertheless makes the point that the distribution of ruses in physical space can have an aggregated effect at the operational or strategic levels of war.

- **Level of sophistication.** As the deceiver's intelligence picture improves, the power or scope of deceptions may increase. The incorporation of new information about the target of the deception (their sensors, preconceptions, history, etc.) or the environment (ambient light and noise levels, terrain type, engagement ranges, etc.) greatly increases the level of sophistication of the deception. Although it has not yet been experimentally demonstrated that level of sophistication correlates with success, it is a reasonable hypothesis. Consider the use of a lure: the angler fish *Lophius piscatorius* has a worm-like bit of webbing on the end of its forward dorsal spine which it bobs about to attract prey. This deception is not terribly specific (the angler preys upon numerous smaller species indiscriminately) but still quite effective. On the other hand, the PIRA often carefully tailored its deception techniques based upon what it knew of British standing operating procedures (SOPs), as Curtis (1998) relates. In one incident, a tractor tire with wires visibly poking out is left outside a betting shop in Brompton Park, Belfast, as a lure. British SOPs demand that the tire be examined by ordnance-disposal personnel and the area secured by troops. Knowing this, and knowing that the soldiery securing the perimeter are likely to be diffusing their attention between outside threats and the disposal operation in their midst, the PIRA forces set a successful ambush, killing one and wounding two. The nature of the lure in this case is based quite specifically upon knowledge of the foe (learned through previous encounters, informers, etc.). Not only are the resulting deceptions more likely to succeed, but the consequences of the deception are made much more deadly. Although this example is tactical, a few such successes that result in significant friendly casualties, well-publicized mission failures, property damage, or third-party misfortunes could have operational- or strategic-level effects.

This principle of accumulating operational or strategic value by combining tactical-level deceptions is eminently visible in a historical review of military deception, which often reveals exactly this sort of aggregation. For example, disparate Egyptian deception measures preparatory to the 1973 surprise attack at the Suez Canal were designed with a specific cumulative effect in mind. *Together* they were meant to create a strategic deception aimed at Israeli intelligence analysts and commanders. The Egyptians demobilized 20,000 troops days before the attack; staged numerous and repeated canal-crossing exercises; used frequent maneuvers and construction activities to cache crossing equipment at hidden depots near the canal; spread a variety of rumors via radio, print, and word of mouth that made an attack seem unlikely; and continued to build *defensive* lines as though settling in for a long haul at these positions (Betts, 1982; Haykal, 1975). It seems fair to say that the strongest doctrinal embrace of this method would be Soviet (now Russian) doctrine of *maskirovka*, which has long espoused that strategic-level benefits will grow from aggregations of tactical- and operational-level deceptions (Glantz, 1989).

COUNTERDECEPTION

[His] voice attempted one final deception: "Thy abominable sins forbid thee to look upon my radiance . . ." he began. No one was listening; he was riddled with spears. (J.L. Borges, *A Universal History of Infamy [The Masked Dyer]*)

The other side of the coin in developing deception theory is counterdeception theory. The authors believe that deception and counterdeception capabilities must not be isolated from one another, but analyzed and developed in a complementary fashion with a significant amount of cross-pollination.

That said, how shall we begin our consideration of counterdeception? As noted above, deception seeks to engender errors in the perceptual apparatus of the target with the goal of causing bad decisions to be made. What comprises the perceptual apparatus of an entity?

*   The intended target of any deception possesses sensory devices (radars, forward-looking infrared radars (FLIR), eyeballs, ears, etc.) . . .

*   which he or she employs in a given method (inch-by-inch scrutiny, quick scans, random walks, spiral searches, etc.) . . .

*   and the resulting data is processed in a certain way (compared en masse to a template, examined completely from scratch, ranked by vividness, etc.).

These three elements of perception comprise a trajectory from sensation to cognition, and each represents a milestone where efforts to shield the entity from deception can be focused.

1. **Type or amount of data collected.** What can be done with the sensor? Can it be tuned to another window of the spectrum (e.g., switching from visible light to infrared)? Can another sensory modality be brought on-line (e.g., switching from visual to auditory searching)?

2. **Method for collecting data.** What can be done to the sensory processing? Can the search *plan* be changed (e.g., from scanning/cueing to inch-by-inch scrutiny)? Can the search *pattern* be changed (e.g., from outward spiraling to sector-by-sector)?

3. **Analysis of data collected.** What can be done with the analysis of sensory inputs? How can thinking help? Can the inputs be corroborated? Can counterscenarios be concocted?

There are other ways in which deception can be combated, as suggested by examples in both military history and the animal kingdom:

4. **Unmasking adversary deceptions with friendly deceptions.** Fighting fire with fire: What deceptive counteractions can be taken? Can bluff or bluster uncover an adversary's deception?

5. **Rendering adversary deceptions moot.** Can the deception or its effects be overwhelmed? That is, can the effects of misperception be mitigated through actions that lessen the importance of accurate perception? For example, if an enemy tank has deployed decoys, this counterstrategy would simply target them all with destructive fires and not bother to tell them apart. Or if an enemy force feints right and comes left, an "overwhelming" response would be to simply respond forcefully at both locations, not bothering to discern which is real. Needless to say, this strategy requires great resources.

How is this typology useful? As with the framework we employ to unpack the deception phenomenon, it is meant to offer a more finely resolved view of a complex issue and thus represent an intermediate step toward creating a comprehensive theory of deception and counterdeception. Table 3 illustrates both military and animal examples of these counterdeception categories.

Table 3

Examples of Counterdeception

Focus	Simple Military Examples	Biological Examples
Type of data collected	Defeat adversary visual camouflage with foliage-penetrating (FOPEN) radar	Insectivorous bats (*chiroptera*) defeat the well-developed visual camouflage of moths by using a different sensory medium: echolocation.
Method for collecting data	Defeat adversary camouflage by modifying current search protocols (e.g., use complementary/corroboratory emitters) or by increasing deliberation	*Photinus* fireflies defeat the aggressive mimicry of *Photuris* fireflies by slowing their approaches and prolonging the time of communication. The deception is often revealed by not acting hastily.
Analysis of data collected	Defeat adversary camouflage by developing improved imagery intelligence (IMINT) analyst techniques and training	Reed warblers defeat cuckoo brood parasitism (mimicry) by applying rules to their nest contents. If an egg doesn't resemble the others closely enough, if the egg appears in the nest too early, or if an adult cuckoo was spotted nearby during the laying period, then the reed warbler is likely to reject an egg.
Unmasking adversary deceptions with friendly deceptions	Defeat adversary camouflage by employing a feint to encourage concealed targets to maneuver	The Boomslang snake (*Dispholidus typus*, pictured in Figure 10; see following page 32) defeats the camouflage of a chameleon by lying in wait and employing its own excellent camouflage. When unaware of danger, the chameleon moves/forages and thus reveals itself to the snake.
Rendering adversary deceptions moot	Defeat adversary camouflage by saturating areas with fire to destroy concealed targets	A variety of avians that feed on butterflies of the *Satyridae* family, geckos, and other species with disposable, diverting body parts (e.g., eye spots on wing tips) strike repeatedly or take large bites, meaning that the deceptions have no impact even when effective.

As discussed previously, the defense community's knowledge is somewhat impoverished when it comes to the specific costs, benefits, risks, optimization points, contextual interrelationships, etc. of deception. This is equally true of counterdeception; the reader should consider the list in Table 4 a counterpart to the one in Table 1.

It seems clear that as much needs to be done on this topic as on deception itself. A key finding emerging from this research is that different counterdeception methods can and should be applied toward different deception techniques. The authors believe that as a starting point, experimentation should be done to define these relationships. Are improvements to analysis (e.g., changes to training) more suited to countering *masking* (e.g., camouflage) techniques than *misdirecting* (e.g., feints) techniques? Even more specific questions can and should be asked: for example, will improvements to sensors fare better against *behavioral* means of masking than *morphological* means of masking? How much better? What level of investment is required in improved training to significantly affect outcomes? As noted previously, there are numerous such questions; the answers will be of great value. A body of thoroughly vetted experimentation and analysis is needed that clearly prescribes what sorts

Table 4

Issues in Countering Deception

Matching up	Which counterdeception methods work against particular types of deception? Why?
Most effective	Which are the most effective against particular deception techniques?
Broadest effectiveness	Which are effective against the broadest range of deceptions?
Context	Which are the most affected by the context of their use?
Time	Which require the most time?
Manpower	Which require the most manpower?
Automation	Which can be automated?
Positive interactions	Which complement each other? Which complement other operational capabilities?
Negative interactions	Which hinder each other?
Monkey's paw	Do any of the methods help against one type of deception but actually incur a vulnerability to another type?

of counterefforts to employ to stave off particular types of deception (or the reverse: if the opponent has x, y, and z intelligence capabilities, then use deceptions a, b, and c).

This entire framework is most useful when considered as a set of hypotheses to be experimentally tested and thoroughly analyzed. If borne out, they could pay significant dividends in driving technological, doctrinal, and organizational change in the U.S. armed forces wherever adversaries are resorting to such measures.

Chapter Five

A COEVOLUTIONARY PERSPECTIVE OF
DECEPTION AND COUNTERDECEPTION

The complex adaptations and counteradaptations we see between predators and their prey are testament to their long coexistence and reflect the result of an arms race over evolutionary time. (Krebs and Davies, 1993)

DECEPTION AS ADAPTATION

CCD [camouflage, concealment, and deception] is less costly than comparable *survivability* alternatives. While CCD and hardening yielded equivalent levels of survivability when attacked by the same system, CCD was always less costly and more quickly employed. (Joint CCD Program FY95 annual report)

In the course of this research, the authors have seen an interesting motif often repeated in descriptions of OPFOR, insurgents, guerrilla fighters, terrorist groups, overmatched conventional combatants, and the like. That theme is one of *adaptation*: of evolving tactics, technologies, targets, group dynamics, and other behaviors. The list of actors that have been characterized in this fashion—that is, by an invocation of biological principles—includes groups spanning the globe, from Northern Ireland, to the Balkans, to the Caucasus, to Kashmir and Sri Lanka, throughout Latin America, across the Pacific Rim, and, not incidentally, within the United States itself (Bell, 1991, 1997; Daalder and O'Hanlon, 2000; Pavkovic, 2000; Lieven, 1998; Gall and De Waal, 1998; Singh, 1999; Schofield, 2000; McCormick, 1990, 1992; Schultz, 1999).

There are numerous ways in which predators and prey adapt, as illustrated by Table 5, where it is easy to see the analogy between the biological and military domains. Though not exhaustive, the table illustrates what should be a familiar pattern to any student of conflict: the cycle of measure and countermeasure development between combatants. This same pattern is visible in numerous cases of human conflict, where descriptors such as "evolutionary," "adaptive," and similar terms were used to characterize the course of a combatant's development.

Note the frequency with which deception (crypsis, mimicry, "startles") appears. Since all entities seek accuracy in their perceptions, and accurate perceptions rely heavily upon the performance of an individual's sensors, improvements to sensors or sensory processing are significant contributors to survival; this is as true for human combatants as it is for any animal in any environment. It should not be surprising, therefore, that the reverse holds true: capabilities that engender *inaccuracy* in the perceptions of the foe (be they attacker or defender) tend to be highly advantageous. As discussed earlier, this capability is defined as *deception*, and the advantage it provides stems from the erroneous action that so often follows from inaccurate perception. As one component of this research, the authors have explored *how* deception capabilities evolve. Doing so supports both of our primary goals: developing better deception TTPs for

Table 5

Co-evolution of Adaptation and Counteradaptation

Activity	Adaptation	Counteradaptation
Searching	Improved visual acuity	Crypsis
	Search image	Polymorphism
	Search limited area where prey abundant	Space out (disperse)
Recognition	Learning	Mimicry
Catching	Crypsis	Improved visual acuity
	Lures, traps	Reconnaissance, learning
	Motor skills (speed, agility)	Escape flights, "startle" response
	Weapons of offense	Weapons of defense
Handling	Subduing skills	Active defense, spines, tough integument
	Toxins	Detoxification ability

NOTE: Drawn from Krebs and Davies (1993).

friendly forces, and prescribing better methods of preventing or countering adversary deceptions. (Note that while the focus of this work remains the role of deception in urban operations, the authors feel strongly that gains made in this area can be exported to other domains of conflict.) So, then, how do adaptations that attack an opponent's perceptual apparatus—that is, deceptions—arise? By this "how" we mean under what circumstances, requiring which resources, and regarding all the other particulars of adaptation.

It seems fair to state that different groups of combatants evolve differently over time. Some adapt to changing circumstances quite quickly; others adapt slowly. Some explicitly spend time investigating new technologies and TTPs; others stick to time-honored or traditional methods that they know best. Some institutionalize the learning process; others rely on on-the-job experience. The authors believe that a profile—which we might call the *adaptive index*—may be used to portray any battlefield element in terms of its *capability, likelihood,* and *swiftness to adapt.* Table 6 contains two very simple illustrations of the principle.

Table 6
Simple Illustrations of the Adaptive Index

Quality Under Scrutiny	Low Adaptive Index	High Adaptive Index
Connectivity; ability for ideas or information to spread through population	*Cellularized insurgent force:* fighters who don't know each other and seldom communicate. A lesson learned or technological advance by one progresses through the population very slowly.	*Intranetted insurgent force:* fighters with superb internal communications. A lesson learned or technological advance by one rapidly spreads through the community.
Propensity for innovation in methods	*Traditionalist insurgent force:* combatants who, whether by ideology or lack of resources, stick to well-established TTPs. Diversity of TTPs looks normally distributed. Innovation arises through natural selection (i.e., whoever survives adversary actions passes along their version of TTP).	*Experimentalist insurgent force:* combatants consider R&D and diversity of TTPs a priority. Diversity of those TTPs has a much flatter and broader distribution (percent of population killed by adversary actions is smaller, and variations in TTPs are greater).

Table 7

Components of the Descriptor Adaptive Index as Applied to a
Subject Group

Diversity	How much baseline heterogeneity exists in the group?
Innovation	How much baseline innovation is occurring?
Forces at work	Is innovation self-directed (i.e., R&D) or other-directed (i.e., natural selection)?
Intensity of forces	How intense are the selective pressures?
Turnover	What is the baseline speed of innovation?
Learning	How well do members of the group learn?
Organization	Does the organization of the group enhance or hinder innovation?
Leadership	Does the leadership embrace innovation or discourage it?
Scope of effort	What is the overall volume of group activity?
Supply	How abundant are needed resources?
Transmission speed	How fast can information travel between members of the group?
Transmission error rate	How much information loss occurs in transmission?

While the descriptions in the table are oversimplified, they should make the point nonetheless: as one side is wargaming the possibilities for adversary courses of action (COA), they ought to take a long, explicit look at the inherent adaptability of any battlefield element as well as the potential for the environment to support adaptation. Consider just one of many critical elements in operations: *time.* If time is long (e.g., in an ongoing peacekeeping operation or drawn-out occupation), an adversary with a high adaptive index is very likely to demonstrate new technical capabilities, new tactics, new target sets, and the like. This is certainly a concern for friendly force commanders. On the other hand, if time is short (e.g., a noncombatant evacuation operation (NEO)), then adversary evolution is likely to be less of a concern.

What intelligence is required to construct an adaptive index? The authors hypothesize that the measure would comprise both endogenous and exogenous factors, a partial list of which may be found in Table 7. (Note that adaptive index as defined here is a *qualitative* descriptor meant to provoke decisionmakers' careful consideration.)

Clearly, answers to the questions in the table are intelligence products; they are the refined outcomes of thorough and competent intelligence analysis. "Adaptive index" would be a term useful to military decisionmakers (at any operational level) in much the same way that the term "fitness" is useful in biology to describe a population and make predictions about likely survivability outcomes given particular perturbations to the equilibrium. That is, a battlefield element's adaptive index could be used in conjunction with other descriptors (e.g., order of battle, cultural intelligence, likely courses of action) in wargaming as a measure of how much any element is likely to advantageously change over time.

COUNTERDECEPTION AS COUNTERADAPTATION

Hezbollah, the Shiite Muslim guerrilla organization that forced Israel from the slice of southern Lebanon it had occupied for 22 years, grew from a small band of amateurish gunmen to a highly sophisticated tactical operation . . . From once relying on teenage suicide bombers to crash cars into Israeli installations in the mid-1980s, Hezbollah tactics—primarily ambushes, assassinations and roadside bombs—became increasingly well planned and executed, military observers in the region say . . . "When they first started, they thought they could do it with a bunch of people on a hill yelling 'Allah-u akbar,'" a United Nations official in the area said of the Hezbollah fighters, "They would lose 40 in an operation. Now they are very sophisticated, very disciplined" . . . In an interview, [the top Hezbollah commander in southern Lebanon] Sheik [Nabil] Qaouk said that the guerrillas had been able to improve their effectiveness by studying each operation, learning from their mistakes and developing new uses for their weaponry. (*The New York Times*, July 19, 2000)

Anyone dumb enough to get killed by a HARM [high-speed anti-radiation missile] is dead already. Everyone left standing is going to innovate with their [integrated air defenses]. (Joint Suppression of Enemy Air Defenses (JSEAD) staff member, discussion with author, May 9, 2000)

As described above, a historically significant form of adaptation is deception, and the authors believe that recognizing this leads to a fruitful area of counterdeception: preventing adversaries from mounting sophisticated deceptions through a systematic program of counteradaptation.

In a word: *friendly actions should be planned with adversary adaptability in mind.* Why? It is wise to engage adversaries with high adaptive indices in such a way to reduce their ability to change. To reuse an earlier example: if preventing the adversary's adaptation is considered a priority, then he should be deined the luxury of time. How is this to be accomplished? Speed: mobility, agility, and quickness should be among the key components of the friendly operation (if feasible). Those components of friendly operations that impede or altogether thwart adversaries from making advantageous adjustments may be called "counteradaptive." Reflecting upon natural selection and adaptation as it occurs in nature, the authors believe that a list of "counteradaptive" measures (including speed) would resemble Table 8 .

Note that this list represents a set of hypotheses to be tested, and it may well turn out that some elements are more or less effective than others in a counteradaptation role. For example, deceiving the enemy as to the success of their methods might delay innovation more than simply shutting down their telecommunications network would do. It is also conceivable that even *effective* counteradaptation measures only contribute a small amount to the variance of this complex phenomenon. For example, an adversarial nation-state may actively pursue R&D irrespective of day-to-day battlefield developments; or a rigidly traditional nonstate actor might eschew innovation for religious reasons.

The authors believe that a model for "thinking counteradaptively" is to be found in Allied management of ULTRA: extreme steps were taken to ensure that Allied decisionmaking did not seem to be a result of code-breaking, and therefore the Germans were not encouraged to alter Enigma (Montagu, 1978). The Special Operations Executive understood that penetration of German codes was an immensely valuable, but precarious, advantage. While the stakes may not be quite so high in contemporary deployments, the model is nevertheless quite instructive. Counteradaptation is a means of

Table 8

**Operational Measures That May Counter or Minimize
Adversary Adaptation**

Element	Counteradaptive Effect
Overwhelming speed	Without enough time to react, it is very difficult to generate, test, evaluate, and field countermeasures. Example: Kuwait City, 1991.
Complete destruction of enemy	A 100% enemy kill leaves no survivors to transmit information about friendly techniques, countermeasures, etc.
Degradation/ destruction of communications infrastructure	If information cannot be transmitted effectively, it is exceedingly difficult for new countermeasures to spread across a population.
OPSEC and deception to protect methods	Often the adversary must gather intelligence about friendly capabilities. The less they know (or the less correct their assessments), the more difficult their job of innovating.
Multiple modes of action	This is essentially an attempt at making the burden of innovation too heavy to bear. If friendly measures are diverse, it forces adversary countermeasures to be similarly diverse—an expense in effort, time, and resources. Moreover, the more complex and varied the countermeasures must be, the more likely it is that some portion of them will be ineffective.
Interdiction of R&D resources	As resources (food, money, sanctuary, personnel, laboratories, etc.) become scarcer, it is increasingly difficult to innovate. This will vary greatly by the type of countermeasure in question; new means of jamming global positioning system (GPS) or spoofing identification friend or foe (IFF) transponders will require more infrastructural resources than new means of using terrain shadows to thwart the joint surveillance, targeting and reconnaissance system (JSTARS).
Deception introduced into enemy adaptation process	Covert/clandestine or other actions taken to introduce errors into the innovation process may significantly hamper adaptation. The possibilities are numerous: disinformation may be placed in the adversary's hands that purports to reveal a GPS vulnerability, or an adversary's tank that is *poorly* camouflaged may be allowed to go unmolested in order to allow replication of the poor procedures by other tanks (and incidentally, in order to discourage innovation).

Table 8—continued

Purposeful unpredictability or built-in randomization	If adversaries have some uncertainty about the friendly force's rules of engagement (ROE), operating parameters, or munition probability-of-kill (P_k), then they are likely to expend more effort in their innovation process and end up with errors in their assessments (and thus fielded countermeasures). The question of how much randomness (r) needs to be injected in order to generate a specified amount of uncertainty (u) is an interesting issue.
Judicious timing and application of methods (see Axelrod, 1979)	In order to experiment broadly, generate heterogeneity, and evaluate results, there usually needs to be a significant volume of activity. If an asset is tightly husbanded and therefore exposure to the adversary is small, then the information gained about the technique may be too little or too late for useful adaptation.

wedging open the adversary's window of vulnerability. Consider, for example, if U.S. forces deployed in an urban peacekeeping venture fielded powerful, portable chemical detectors that tremendously improved bomb-sniffing capabilities. An adaptive enemy would soon find ways of either jamming the devices, spoofing them, or overloading them, or they would simply resort to new bomb-placement strategies, requiring new innovations by friendly forces, and so forth. The commander ordering the deployment of such devices in the first place would be well advised to consider adversary adaptability upon deployment. What is the time frame of the operation? What resources are available to the adversary? How good is adversary intelligence gathering with respect to friendly capabilities? How fast does news spread in-theater? How is the adversary's organization structured? Do they have a history of innovation? Have we penetrated their communications? These and other questions could provide intelligence of significant prescriptive value. Perhaps every bomb discovery should be loudly attributed to means other than this new chemical sensor. Alternately, friendly forces could conveniently "misplace" a false sensor to be discovered and reverse-engineered by the adversary. A third counteradaptive strategy might be to husband the sensor and then employ it aggressively, widely, and in an acute time frame, perhaps even coupled with martial law or other drastic measures (the goal of this third strategy would be to virtually eliminate adversary adaptation over a short interval, as opposed to the previous two strategies, the goal of which would be to suppress adversary adaptation over a longer period).

Chapter Six

CONCLUSIONS

What does all of this analysis mean for urban operations? How do these observations, principles, and theoretic constructs apply to the soldiers, marines, and airmen who must execute their missions in the dense, chaotic terrain of a city or other built-up area? The authors' goals in this research on deception were twofold: (1) to broaden and deepen current theory and (2) to identify new possibilities for innovation and experimentation. We believe that there are several reasonable propositions that stem from this analysis, any and all of which will support U.S. deployments into the urban environment.

Deception, in all of its myriad forms, should be made a primary instrument of both force multiplication and force protection.

Deception techniques should be cultivated in our soldiery (on both the technology and training sides) with the same level of emphasis we place on basic firearms skills. In the course of our research into animal biology, we have come to believe that deception is an adaptation as valuable as armor, speed, or firepower. Deception is ubiquitous and enduring, whether in the form of masking one's presence, diverting an opponent's attention for a critical few seconds, paralyzing an adversary with uncertainty, or any of countless other effects. In the unforgiving regime of natural selection, deception's longevity and ubiquity are themselves arguments supporting their great worth. While many or most in the defense community would concur with this assertion, it has not translated into action. Deception is given short shrift in terms of the time soldiers spend learning or practicing the art of the ruse. Yet in interviews with soldiers, marines or other servicemen, deception is deemed a life-saver and a singular source of achieving surprise against the adversary. The authors strongly believe that the United States ought to apply resources to turn clever ideas and novel technologies into deceptive shaping actions on the battlefield, at any level of war. Doing so would be of incalculable value in the urban jungle. Examining just the few lessons cited in this report—active motion camouflage, employing multiple deceptions for aggregate effect, and infiltration/subversion of enemy-held terrain—demonstrates that there are numerous new paths to be explored in both technological development as well as doctrinal improvement. Urban terrain is an environment eminently suited to deception, and this assertion is borne out fully by the historical record. For U.S. forces not to receive the training or tools to leverage the environment as well as or better than our adversaries do is a sorely missed opportunity. The first locations that a renewed commitment to deception should be made manifest are in experiments, exercises, and simulations. In current simulations, for example, there is a lamentable lack of deception capabilities built in for any element, which is dramatically at odds with the historical reality of urban operations.

Counterdeception TTPs must be improved.

The authors see this as a critical component to urban reconnaissance. Urban terrain takes a toll on situational awareness through the degradation of sensors and communications, the presence of large numbers of noncombatants and dense infrastructure, and the high-OPTEMPO characteristic of urban operations. Yet our adversaries will seek to degrade U.S. forces' situational awareness beyond the injury inflicted by the urban terrain itself. Their efforts to do so will include deception: using camouflage, decoys, deliberately confusing maneuvers (feints and demonstrations), and disinformative HUMINT and SIGINT, to name just a few methods. It is critical to note that *improvements to reconnaissance instruments do not necessarily yield improvements to counterdeception capabilities.* As discussed previously, lowering the detection threshold of a particular sensor to find hidden (camouflaged) foes may allow those same foes to simply begin generating false positives (decoys). The outcomes for U.S. forces might well be worsened as a result. Counterdeception is a skill set that is *distinct from,* though complementary to, reconnaissance methods. Counterdeception capabilities should be diverse and robust, developed alongside reconnaissance TTPs to match the varied deceptions of a particular foe. If an adversary's use of deception can be considered an element of counterreconnaissance, then a coevolutionary perspective on counterdeception suggests that reconnaissance TTPs must be adapted in synchrony with an adversary's deceptive innovations. In practice, this means exploiting the whole range of counterdeception possibilities as explored in Chapter Four: improving and diversifying sensors, training combatants to think about the intelligence they receive in new ways, giving combatants deceptive capabilities with which they might unmask the ruses of their adversaries, and drafting operational plans (OPLANS) that render moot the subterfuges of the adversary. Moreover, as described in Chapter Five, OPLANS that prevent the development or employment of deception by the adversary are highly desirable and can be seen as striking against the enemy's capability to adapt.

It would be wise to encourage diversity and flexibility in our own units' urban training.

The authors strongly believe that good doctrine and TTPs should be flexible and allow for adaptation as the circumstances warrant. While standardization is indisputably valuable, there is also demonstrable value to deliberately embracing diversity. *Diversity is an essential component of adaptation,* and adaptation is likely to be as valuable for friendly forces as it is worrisome when seen in the adversary. Consider U.S. military exercises and experiments, where one unit portraying U.S. or allied forces (termed BLUFOR) trains against another unit portraying opposing forces (termed OPFOR). In exercises and training, it is the OPFOR that all too often adapts more quickly and more effectively than the BLUFOR. Why? The OPFOR is unconstrained relative to the BLUFOR, and thus it is free to innovate. Moreover, the innovation occurs at a more atomic level than in the BLUFOR, meaning that small groups of OPFOR are using somewhat *different* TTPs at any given time. As the success or failure of those different TTPs becomes disseminated, the lack of constraints allows rapid adoption by other units. BLUFOR's rigidity means that adaptation is slow, while the OPFOR's liberty yields more expeditious evolution. Parenthetically, while the advantageous adaptations we refer to could be in any area—mobility, situational awareness, communications, weapon use—many of the observed beneficial adaptations were, not surprisingly, deceptive. That is, the OPFOR learned how to improve its concealment and its diversions, how to aggregate deceptions together for greater effect, and so on. Deception in urban operations is usually inexpensive and yet very effective. The authors believe that some consideration should be given to generating more incentives and greater resources for BLUFOR to innovate and adapt, particularly in deceptive methods. While it is clearly not without risk, it may prove immensely valuable for BLUFOR to *plan on adapting*, particularly if they are given the resources to do so. For example, a multispectral close-combat decoy (MCCD) can be used in a thousand clever ways, and only a tiny few of those ways will be apparent before the battle has been joined. The authors are impressed with the ingenuity of our servicemen and women. Providing BLUFOR with some general capabilities that might be invoked *on the fly* could well allow friendly forces to adapt as quickly as the OPFOR does. At the least, the authors believe that soldiers, marines, and other servicemen training for urban operations should be encouraged to innovate and adapt their methods and equipment. With regard to deception-type adaptations by company-size or smaller units, the authors believe that in exercises and experiments the risks and deconfliction requirements can be fully explored.

Prevent adversaries from adapting when possible, but stay abreast or ahead of adversary adaptation when prevention is infeasible.

This is probably a useful exhortation in general—we would certainly prefer that adversaries not field new weapons, effectively innovate in their tactics, and so forth—but it is especially true for deception, and even more so in urban terrain. As adversaries learn the extent of friendly ROE, the specifics of the friendly order of battle, and otherwise enrich their intelligence picture generally, they will almost certainly innovate to exploit such knowledge. Moreover, the dense and resource-rich urban environment supports innovation in general to an extent that a desert or jungle never could. As the authors have argued previously, these resources allow for a multitude of deceptive adaptations not possible in other environments. Combatants take advantage of telecommunications equipment to produce bogus communications intelligence (COMINT) and SIGINT; the civilian population, the journalistic media, and other NGOs are used to disseminate false HUMINT; civilian vehicles and mannequins can be used to create decoys; and on and on. As detailed in Chapter Five, the authors believe that a systematic effort to suppress adversary adaptation could be the single most effective counterdeception technique available. An adversary who cannot effectively adapt, or is precluded from doing so, is headed for impotence and extinction and, therefore, far less likely to represent a hindrance to friendly force missions and a hazard to friendly personnel.

A better understanding of deception carries important technological implications.

History suggests that deceptions that are added as an afterthought are at best marginally useful. Deception is most effective when it is integrated into planning from the outset. As plans are drawn up for the IBCT and Objective Force, including for example the Future Combat Systems, next-generation communications equipment, multispectral close-combat decoys, or battle dress uniforms, improvements in the science of deception will figure prominently in those designs. Given the enhanced survivability of organisms that employ well-tailored deceptions, it would appear that investment in deception science is extremely worthwhile.

BIBLIOGRAPHY

Agosta, W. (2001). *Thieves, Deceivers, and Killers.* Princeton, NJ: Princeton University Press.

Allen, C. (1990). *The Savage Wars of Peace: Soldiers' Voices 1945–1989.* London: Michael Joseph.

Anderson, C., Lepper, M., and Ross, L. (1980). "Perseverance of Social Theories: The Role of Explanation in the Persistence of Discredited Information." *Journal of Personality and Social Psychology,* 39:1037–1049.

Asprey, R. (1994). *War in the Shadows: The Guerrilla in History.* New York: Morrow.

Axelrod, R. (1979). "The Rational Timing of Surprise." *World Politics,* 31(2):228–246.

Bateson, G. (1972). "The Logical Categories of Learning and Communication." In Bateson, *Steps to an Ecology of Mind.* New York: Ballantine Books.

Baumann, M. (1975). *Wie Alles Anfing?* [Terror or Love?] New York: Grove Press.

Begin, M. (1972). *The Revolt.* Los Angeles: Nash Publications.

Bell, J.B., and Whaley, B. (1991). *Cheating and Deception.* New Brunswick: Transaction Publishers.

Bell, J.B. (1991). *IRA Tactics and Targets: An Analysis of Tactical Aspects of the Armed Struggle 1969–1989*. New Brunswick: Transaction Publishers.

Bell, J.B. (1997). *The Secret Army: The IRA*. New Brunswick: Transaction Publishers.

Betts, R. (1982). *Surprise Attack: Lessons for Defense Planning*. Washington, D.C.: The Brookings Institution.

Blum, R. (1972). *Deceivers and Deceived: Observations on Confidence Men and Their Victims, Informants and Their Quarry, Political and Individual Spies and Ordinary Citizens*. Illinois: C.C. Thomas.

Brower, L. (1969). "Ecological Chemistry." *Scientific American*, 220(2):22–29.

Brown, L., and Amadon, D. (1968). *Eagles, Hawks, and Falcons of the World*. Feltham: Country Life Books.

Christmas, R. (1977). "A Company Commander Remembers the Battle for Hue." *Marine Corps Gazette*, February.

Cohen, S. (1978). "Environmental Load and Allocation of Attention." In A. Baum, J. Singer, and S. Valins (eds.), *Advances in Environmental Psychology*, vol. 1. New York: Halstead Press.

Collins, E. (1997). *Killing Rage*. London: Granta Books.

Collett, T., and Land, M. (1978). "How Hoverflies Compute Interception Courses." *Journal of Comparative Physiology*, 125:191–204.

Cott, H. (1966). *Adaptive Coloration in Animals*, 3rd edition. London: Methuen & Co.

Courand, G. (1989). *Counter Deception*. Mountain View, CA: Advanced Decision Systems.

Cruickshank, C. (1979). *Deception in World War Two*. New York: Oxford University Press.

Curio, E. (1976). *The Ethology of Predation*. Berlin: Springer-Verlag.

Curtis, N. (1998). *Faith and Duty*. London: Andre Deutsch.

Daalder, I., and O'Hanlon, M. (2000). *Winning Ugly: NATO's War to Save Kosovo.* Washington, D.C.: The Brookings Institution.

Daniel, D., and Herbig, K. (1982). *Strategic Military Deception.* New York: Pergamon Press.

Davies, N., and Brooke, M. (1988). "Cuckoos Versus Reed Warblers: Adaptations and Counter-Adaptations." *Animal Behaviour,* 36:262–284.

Davies, N., and Brooke, M. (1989a). "An Experimental Study of Coevolution Between the Cuckoo *Cuculus canorus* and Its Hosts. I. Egg Discrimination." *Journal of Animal Ecology,* 58:207–224.

Davies, N., and Brooke, M. (1989b). "An Experimental Study of Coevolution Between the Cuckoo *Cuculus canorus* and Its Hosts. II. Host Egg Markings, Chick Discrimination, and General Discussion." *Journal of Animal Ecology,* 58:225–236.

Dawkins, M. (1971). "Perceptual Changes in Chicks: Another Look at the 'Search Image' Concept." *Animal Behaviour,* 19:566–574.

Dawkins, R., and Krebs, J. (1978). "Animal Signals: Information or Manipulation?" In J. Krebs and N. Davies (eds.), *Behavioral Ecology: An Evolutionary Approach.* Oxford: Blackwell Scientific, 282–309.

Dawkins, R., and Krebs, J. (1979). "Arms Races Between and Within Species." *Proceedings of the Royal Society of London, Series B,* 205: 489–511.

Dewar, M. (1989). *The Art of Deception in Warfare.* Newton Abbot, Devon: David & Charles.

Dewar, M. (1992). *War in the Streets: The Story of Urban Combat from Calais to Khafji.* Newton Abbot, Devon: David & Charles.

Donnelly, T., Roth, M., and Baker, C. (1991). *Operation Just Cause: The Storming of Panama.* New York: Lexington Books.

Dunnigan, J., and Nofi, A. (1995). *Victory and Deceit: Dirty Tricks at War.* New York: W. Morrow.

Eagly, A., Wood, W., and Chaiken, S. (1978). "Causal Inferences About Communicators and Their Effect on Opinion Change." *Journal of Personality and Social Psychology*, 36:424–435.

Edwards, Sean J.A. (2001). *Freeing Mercury's Wings: Improving Tactical Communications in Cities.* Santa Monica, CA: RAND, MR-1316-A.

Eldredge, N. (1980). "An Extravagance of Species: The Diversity of Fossil Trilobites Poses a Challenge to Traditional Evolutionary Theory." *Natural History*, 89(7):46–51.

Ellefsen, D. (1987). *Urban Terrain Zone Characteristics.* Aberdeen Proving Ground: U.S. Army Human Engineering Labs.

Endler, J. (1980). "Natural Selection on Color Patterns in Poecilia Reticulata." *Evolution*, 34:76–91.

Endler, J. (1983). "Natural and Sexual Selection on Color Patterns in Poeciliid Fishes." *Environmental Biology of Fishes*, 9:173–190.

Endler, J. (1991). "Interactions Between Predators and Prey." In J. Krebs and N. Davies (eds.), *Behavioural Ecology: An Evolutionary Approach.* Boston: Blackwell Scientific Publications, pp. 169–196.

Endler, J. (1992). "Signals, Signal Conditions, and the Direction of Evolution." *American Naturalist*, 139 (Supplement):125–153.

Erichsen, J., Krebs, J., and Houston, A. (1980). "Optimal Foraging and Cryptic Prey." *Journal of Animal Ecology*, 49:271–276.

Farnham, D.E. (1988). "Logic for Intelligence Analysts." In R. Garst (ed.), *A Handbook of Intelligence Analysis.* Defense Intelligence College.

Fein, S., Hilton, J., and Miller, D. (1990). "Suspicion of Ulterior Motivation and Correspondence Bias." *Journal of Personality and Social Psychology*, 58:753–764.

Fein, S., and Hilton, J. (1994). "Judging Others in the Shadow of Suspicion." *Motivation and Emotion*, 18:167–198.

Gall, C., and De Waal, T. (1998). *Chechnya: Calamity in the Caucasus.* New York: New York University Press.

George, A. (1972). "The Case for Multiple Advocacy in Making Foreign Policy." *American Political Science Review*, 66.

George, A. (1993). "The Role of Knowledge in Policy-Making." In A. George (ed.), *Bridging the Gap: Theory and Practice in Foreign Policy*. Washington, D.C.: U.S. Institute of Peace Press.

Gerwehr, S., and Glenn, R. (2000). *The Art of Darkness: Deception and Urban Operations*. Santa Monica, CA: RAND, MR-1132-A.

Gilbert, D., and Jones, E. (1986). "Perceiver-Induced Constraint: Interpretations of Self-Generated Reality." *Journal of Personality and Social Psychology*, 50:269–280.

Gittleman, J., and Harvey, P. (1980). "Why Are Distasteful Prey Not Cryptic?" *Nature*, 286:149–150.

Glantz, D. (1989). *Soviet Military Deception in the Second World War*. London: Frank Cass.

Glenn, R. (1996). *Combat in Hell: A Consideration of Constrained Urban Warfare*. Santa Monica, CA: RAND, MR-780-A.

Glenn, R. (1998). *Marching Under Darkening Skies: The American Military and the Impending Urban Operations Threat*. Santa Monica, CA: RAND, MR-1007-A.

Glenn, R. (1999). *". . . We Band of Brothers": The Call for Joint Urban Operations Doctrine*. Santa Monica, CA: RAND, DB-270-JS/A.

Goldthwaite, R., Coss, R., and Owings, D. (1990). "Evolutionary Dissipation of an Antisnake System: Differential Behavior by California and Arctic Ground Squirrels in Above- and Below-Ground Contexts." *Behavior*, 112:246–269.

Greenberg, I. (1982). "Role of Deception in Decision Theory." *Journal of Conflict Resolution*, 26/1:139–156.

Guilford, T. (1986). "How Do 'Warning Colors' Work? Conspicuousness May Reduce Recognition Errors in Experienced Predators." *Animal Behaviour*, 34:286–288.

Guilford, T., and Dawkins, M. (1991). "Receiver Psychology and the Evolution of Animal Signals." *Animal Behaviour*, 39:706–716.

Hammel, E. (1985). *The Root: The Marines in Beirut, August 1982– February 1984.* San Diego: Harcourt Brace Jovanovich.

Hammel, E. (1991). *Fire in the Streets: The Battle for Hue, Tet 1968.* Chicago: Contemporary Books.

Handel, M. (1985). *Military Deception in Peace and War.* Jerusalem: Hebrew University.

Harris, W. (1970). "Counter-Deception Planning: Strategy and Organization." Unpublished RAND research.

Hartcup, G. (1979). *Camouflage: A History of Concealment and Deception in War.* North Pomfret, Vermont: David & Charles.

Hass, R., and Grady, K. (1975). "Temporal Delay, Type of Warning, and Resistance to Influence." *Journal of Experimental Social Psychology,* 11:459–469.

Haykal, M. (1975). *The Road to Ramadan.* New York: New York Times Book Co.

Herek, G., Janis, I., and Huth, P. (1987). "Decision-Making During International Crises: Is Quality of Process Related to Outcome?" *Journal of Conflict Resolution,* 31(2):203–226.

Hilton, J., Fein, S., and Miller, D. (1993). "Suspicion and Dispositional Inference." *Personality and Social Psychology Bulletin,* 19:501–512.

Hoffman, B. (1997). "Why Terrorists Don't Claim Credit." *Terrorism and Political Violence,* 9(1):1–6.

Holldobler, B. (1971). "Communication Between Ants and Their Guests." *Scientific American,* 224:86–93.

Houde, A., and Endler, J. (1990). "Correlated Evolution of Female Mating Preferences and Male Color Patterns in the Guppy Poecilia Reticulata." *Science,* 248:1405–1408.

Jaber, H. (1997). *Hezbollah: Born with a Vengeance.* New York: Columbia University Press.

Janis, I., and Mann, L. (1977). *Decisionmaking: A Psychological Analysis of Conflict, Choice, and Commitment.* New York: Free Press.

Janis, I. (1989). *Crucial Decisions: Leadership in Policy-Making and Management.* New York: Free Press.

Jenkins, B. (1971). *The Five Stages of Urban Guerrilla Warfare: Challenges of the 1970s.* Santa Monica, CA: RAND, P-4670.

Jervis, R. (1968). "Hypotheses on Misperception." *World Politics,* 20(3):454–479.

Jervis, R. (1976). *Perception and Misperception in International Politics.* Princeton, NJ: Princeton University Press.

Johnston, T., and Turvey, M. (1980). "A Sketch of an Ecological Metatheory for Theories of Learning." *Psychology of Learning and Motivation,* 14:147–205.

Kacha, P., and Petr, V. (1995). "Camouflage and Mimicry in Fossils." *Acta Musei Nationalis Pragae, Ser. B, Historia Naturalium,* 51(1–4):53–82.

Kahneman, D., and Tversky, A. (1983). "Choices, Values, Frames." *American Psychologist,* 39(4):341–350.

Kelley, H. (1973). "The Processes of Causal Attribution." *American Psychologist,* 28:107–128.

Koehler, D. (1991). "Explanation, Imagination, and Confidence in Judgement." *Psychological Bulletin,* 110:499–519.

Krebs, J., and Davies, N. (1993). *Introduction to Behavioral Ecology,* 3rd ed. Oxford: Blackwell.

Kruglanski, A. (1987). "Motivation Effects in the Social Comparison of Opinions." *Journal of Personality and Social Psychology,* 53:834–842.

Lambert, D.R. (1987). *A Cognitive Model for the Exposition of Human Deception and Counterdeception.* Washington, D.C.: Naval Materiel Command, NOSC TR 1076.

Lamont, A. (1967). "Environmental Significance of Eye-Reduction in Trilobites and Recent Arthropods: Additional Remarks." *Marine Geology,* 5:377–378.

Lamont, A. (1969). "Prolegomena To Aggressive Mimicry And Protective Resemblance In Early Fishes, Chelicerates, Trilobites And Brachiopods." *Scottish Journal of Science,* 1(2):75–103.

Lieven, A. (1998). *Chechnya: Tombstone of Russian Power.* New Haven, CT: Yale University Press.

Lloyd, J. (1975). "Aggressive Mimicry in Photuris Fireflies: Signal Repertoires by Femmes Fatales." *Science,* 187:452–453.

Lloyd, M. (1997). *The Art of Military Deception.* London: Leo Cooper.

Lotem, A., Nakamura, H., and Zahavi, A. (1992). "Rejection of Cuckoo Eggs in Relation to Host Age: A Possible Evolutionary Equilibrium." *Behavioral Ecology,* 3:128–132.

Marighella, C. (1968). "Mini-Manual of the Urban Guerrilla." In R. Moss, *Urban Guerrilla Warfare.* London: Adelphi Paper No. 79.

Mathtech Inc. (1980). *Deception Maxims, Fact and Folklore.* Washington, D.C.: Office of Research and Development, Central Intelligence Agency.

Matsulenko, V. (1974). "Operativnaya maskirovka voisk v kontranastuplenii pod Stalingradom" [Operational Maskirovka of Forces at Stalingrad]. *VIZh,* No. 1, January.

May, R., and Robinson, S. (1985). "Population Dynamics of Avian Brood Parasitism." *American Naturalist,* 126:475–484.

McCleskey, E. (1991). *Applying Deception to Special Operations Direct Action Missions.* Washington, D.C.: Defense Intelligence College.

McConnell, M. (1991). *Just Cause.* New York: St. Martin's Press.

McCormick, G. (1990). *The Shining Path and the Future of Peru.* Santa Monica, CA: RAND, R-3781-DOS/OSD.

McCormick, G. (1992). *From the Sierra to the Cities: The Urban Campaign of the Shining Path.* Santa Monica, CA: RAND, R-4150-USDP.

McGuire, W., and Papageorgis, D. (1962). "Effectiveness of Forewarning in Developing Resistance to Persuasion." *Public Opinion Quarterly,* 26:24–34.

McLaurin, R.D., and Snider, L.W. (1982*). Recent Military Operations in Urban Terrain.* Aberdeen Proving Ground: U.S. Army Human Engineering Labs.

Menzel, E. (1974). "A Group of Young Chimpanzees in a One-Acre Field." In A. Schrier and F. Stollnitz (eds*.), Behavior of Nonhuman Primates: Modern Research Trends, Vol. 5.* New York: Academic Press.

Milgram, S. (1970). "The Experience of Living in Cities." *Science,* 13:1461–1468.

Miller, J. (1980). "Urban Terrorism in Uruguay: The Tupamaros." In B. O'Neill, W. Heaton, and D. Alberts (eds.), *Insurgency in the Modern World.* Boulder, CO: Westview Press.

Mitchell, R. (1986). "A Framework for Discussing Deception." In R. Mitchell and N. Thompson (eds.), *Deception: Perspectives on Human and Nonhuman Deceit.* New York: SUNY Press.

Moksnes, A., Roskaft, E., Braa, A., Korsnes, L., Lampe, H., and Pedersen, H. (1991). "Behavioral Responses of Potential Hosts Towards Artificial Cuckoo Eggs and Dummies." *Behavior,* 116:64–89.

Monmonier, M. (1996). *How To Lie With Maps.* Chicago: University of Chicago Press.

Montagu, E. (1978). *Beyond Top-Secret Ultra.* New York: Coward, McCann, Geoghegan.

New York Times (1999). "Serb Is Killed in Gun Battle with Marines," June 23.

New York Times (1999). "Damage to Serb Military Less Than Expected," June 27.

New York Times (2000). "In Long Fight with Israel, Hezbollah Tactics Evolved," July 19.

New York Times (2000). "Wasp Invades a Spider and Puts It to Work," July 25.

O'Neill, B., Heaton, W., and Alberts, D. (eds.) (1980). *Insurgency in the Modern World.* Boulder, CO: Westview Press.

Owen, D. (1980). *Camouflage and Mimicry.* Chicago: University of Chicago Press.

Owings, D., and Coss, R. (1977). "Snake Mobbing by California Ground Squirrels: Adaptive Variation and Ontogeny." *Behaviour,* 62:50–69.

Papageorgis, D. (1968). "Warning and Persuasion." *Psychological Bulletin,* 70:271–282.

Pavkovic, A. (2000). *The Fragmentation of Yugoslavia: Nationalism and War in the Balkans.* New York: St. Martin's Press.

Petty, R., and Cacciopo, J. (1977). "Forewarning, Cognitive Responding, and Resistance to Persuasion." *Journal of Personality and Social Psychology,* 35:645–655.

Pietrewicz, A., and Kamil, A. (1981). "Search Images and the Detection of Cryptic Prey: An Operant Approach." In A. Kamil and T. Sargent (eds.), *Foraging Behavior: Ecological, Ethological, and Psychological Approaches,* pp. 311–332. New York: Garland STPM Press.

Poran, N., and Coss, R. (1990). "Development of Antisnake Defences in California Ground Squirrels Spermophilus beechyi: I. Behavioral and Immunological Relationships." *Behaviour,* 112:222–245.

Pratkanis, A., and Aronson, E. (2001). *Age of Propaganda: The Everyday Use and Abuse of Persuasion.* New York: W.H. Freeman & Co.

Rapoport, D. (1997). "To Claim or Not To Claim; That Is the Question—Always!" *Terrorism and Political Violence,* 9(1):11–17.

Rohwer, S., and Spaw, C. (1988). "Evolutionary Lag Versus Bill-Size Constraints: a Comparative Study of the Acceptance of Cowbird Eggs by Old Hosts." *Evolutionary Ecology*, 2:27–36.

Roper, T., and Redston, S. (1987). "Conspicuousness of Distasteful Prey Affects the Strength and Durability of One-Trial Avoidance Learning." *Animal Behaviour*, 35:739–747.

Ross, L., and Anderson, C. (1982). "Shortcomings in Attribution Processes: On the Origins and Maintenance of Erroneous Social Judgements." In D. Kahneman, P. Slovic, and A. Tversky (eds.), *Judgement Under Uncertainty: Heuristics and Biases*. New York: Cambridge University Press.

Rothstein, S. (1974). "Mechanisms of Avian Egg Recognition: Possible Learned and Innate Factors." *Auk*, 91:796–807.

Rothstein, S. (1982). "Mechanisms of Avian Egg Recognition: Which Eggs Elicit Responses by Rejector Species?" *Behavioral Ecology and Sociobiology*, 11:229–239.

Rothstein, S. (1990). "A Model System for Coevolution: Avian Brood Parasitism." *Annual Review of Ecology and Systematics*, 21:481–508.

Royama, T. (1970). "Factors Governing the Hunting Behavior and Selection of Food by the Great Tit, Parus major." *Journal of Animal Ecology*, 39:619–668.

Rue, L. (1994). *By The Grace of Guile*. New York: Oxford University Press.

Sargent, T. (1981). "Antipredator Adaptations of Underwing Moths." In A. Kamil and T. Sargent (eds.), *Foraging Behavior: Ecological, Ethological, and Psychological Approaches*, pp. 259–284. New York: Garland STPM Press.

Schecter, G., and Farrar, D. (1983). *Camouflage in Built Up Areas*. McLean, VA: McLean Research Center. DTIC ADB074334.

Schlenoff, D. (1985). "The Startle Responses of Blue Jays to Catocala (Lepidoptera: Noctuidae) Prey Models." *Animal Behaviour*, 33:1057–1067.

Schofield, V. (2000). *Kashmir in Conflict: India, Pakistan, and the Unfinished War.* London, New York: I.B. Tauris.

Schul, Y., Burnstein, E., and Martinez, J. (1983). "The Informational Basis of Social Judgements: Under What Conditions are Inconsistent Trait Descriptions Processed as Easily as Consistent Ones?" *European Journal of Social Psychology,* 13:143–151.

Schul, Y., and Burnstein, E. (1985). "When Discounting Fails: Conditions Under Which Individuals Use Discredited Information in Making a Judgement." *Journal of Personality and Social Psychology,* 49:894–903.

Schul, Y., and Mazursky, D. (1990). "Conditions Facilitating Successful Discounting in Consumer Decision-Making." *Journal of Consumer Research,* 16:442–451.

Schul, Y. (1993). "When Warning Succeeds: The Effect of Warning on Success of Ignoring Invalid Information." *Journal of Experimental Social Psychology,* 29:42–62.

Schul, Y., Burnstein, E., and Bardi, A. (1996). "Dealing with Deceptions That Are Difficult to Detect: Encoding and Judgement as a Function of Preparing to Receive Invalid Information." *Journal of Experimental Social Psychology,* 32:228–253.

Schultz, R. (1999). *The Secret War Against Hanoi.* New York: Harper-Collins.

Singh, J. (1999). *Kargil 1999: Pakistan's Fourth War for Kashmir.* New Delhi: Knowledge World.

Slatkin, M., and Maynard Smith, J. (1979). "Models of Coevolution." *Quarterly Review of Biology,* 54:233–263.

Smith, S. (1977). "Coral Snake Pattern Rejection and Stimulus Generalization by Naive Great Kiskadees (Aves: Tyrannidae)." *Nature,* 265:535–536.

Snyder, M., and Jones, E. (1974). "Attitude Attribution When Behavior Is Constrained." *Journal of Experimental Social Psychology,* 10:585–600.

Soler, M., and Moller, A. (1990). "Duration of Sympatry and Coevolution Between the Great Spotted Cuckoo and its Magpie Host." *Nature*, 343:748–750.

Srinivasan, M., and Davey, M. (1995). "Strategies for Active Camouflage of Motion." *Proceedings of the Royal Society of London, Series B*, 259:19–25.

Stanley, R. (1998). *To Fool a Glass Eye: Camouflage Versus Photoreconnaissance in WWII*. Washington, D.C.: Smithsonian.

Stebbins, R. (1975). "Putting People On: Deception of Our Fellow Man in Everyday Life." *Sociology and Social Research*, 59(3):189–200.

Taw, J., and Hoffman, B. (1994). *The Urbanization of Insurgency: The Potential Challenge to U.S. Army Operations*. Santa Monica, CA: RAND, MR-398-A.

Tetlock, P., Peterson, R., McGuire, C., Chang, S., and Feld, P. (1992). "Assessing Political Group Dynamics: A Test of the Groupthink Model." *Journal of Personality and Social Psychology*, 63(3):403–425.

Thomas, T. (1997). *The Caucasus Conflict and Russian Security: The Russian Armed Forces Confront Chechnya, I, II, III*. Fort Leavenworth, KS: U.S. Army Foreign Military Studies Office.

Thulborn, T. (1994). "Mimicry in Ankylosaurid Dinosaurs." *Records of the South Australian Museum*, 27(2):151–158.

Tinbergen, L. (1960). "The Natural Control of Insects in Pinewoods. I. Factors Influencing the Intensity of Predation by Song Birds." *Archs. Neerl. Zool*, 13:265–343.

Tversky, A., and Kahneman, D. (1971). The Belief in the Law of Small Numbers. Psychological Bulletin 76: 105–110.

Tversky, A., and Kahneman, D. (1974). "Judgment Under Uncertainty: Heuristics and Biases." *Science*, 185:4157.

United States Army (1988). *Battlefield Deception*, Field Manual 90-2.

United States Air Force, Headquarters (2000). *The Air War Over Serbia: Aerospace Power in Operation Allied Force.*

United States Defense Department Joint Camouflage, Concealment, and Deception Program (1995). *DOT&E annual report.*

United States Joint Publication 1-02 (1993): *DoD Dictionary of Military and Associated Terms.*

United States Joint Publication 3-58 (1996): *Joint Doctrine for Military Deception.*

Vinogradov, B. (1995). "Moscow Has Stated: Military Phase Is Over, Fighting in Grozny Continues." *Izvestiya,* January 21, p. 1.

Whaley, B. (1969). *Stratagem: Deception and Surprise in War.* Cambridge: MIT Center for International Studies.

Whaley, B. (1982). "Toward a General Theory of Deception." In J. Gooch and A. Perlmutter (eds.), *Military Deception and Strategic Surprise.* London: Frank Cass.

Wickler, W. (1968). *Mimicry in Plants and Animals.* New York: McGraw-Hill.